Healthy Eating on a Plate

Healthy Eating on a Plate

Six easy steps to a healthier diet

Janette Marshall

VERMILION

First published in 1995

1 3 5 7 9 10 8 6 4 2

First published in the United Kingdom in 1995 by Vermilion
an imprint of Ebury Press
Random House · 20 Vauxhall Bridge Road · London SW1V 2SA

Random House Australia (Pty) Limited
20 Alfred Street · Milsons Point · Sydney · New South Wales 2061 · Australia

Random House New Zealand Limited
18 Poland Road · Glenfield
Auckland 10 · New Zealand

Random House South Africa (Pty) Limited
PO Box 337 · Bergvlei · South Africa

Random House UK Limited Reg. No. 954009

A CIP catalogue record for this book is available from the British Library.

Printed in England by Clays Ltd, St Ives plc

ISBN: 0 09 180857 X

Papers used by Vermilion are natural, recyclable
products made from wood grown in sustainable forest.

Contents

Acknowledgements
Recommendations throughout this book and
various tables are based on, or taken from

The National Food Guide,
HEALTH EDUCATION AUTHORITY 1994

Nutritional Aspects of Cardiovascular Disease
COMA 1994

Weaning and The Weaning Diet
COMA 1994

INTRODUCTION

The Antidote to Diets

At last! Here is the book that tells you exactly what you need to eat in order to achieve a healthy diet and keep in perfect shape.

No more vague exhortations to 'eat less fat', 'eat less sugar' or 'eat more fibre'. No more wishy-washy, general statements about eating more vegetables and fruit and more starchy foods. Whatever your age and whatever you do for a living, here is the information to select exactly the right amount of the right foods to put on your plate.

- There is no need to cut out any of your favourite foods.
- There is no need to go hungry.
- There is no baffling or contradictory nutritional advice.

This simple and positive programme even encourages you to eat *more* of certain foods. And there's a plan to suit everyone, whether you are an active person or a couch potato.

Everyone can eat themselves into shape

Once you have understood how to make a balanced choice of foods, you can tuck in and let the food on your plate help shape your health and fitness.

The principle is very simple. All you do is balance your food choices to match the healthy eating plate model shown over the page. This illustrates the five food groups and how to choose from them.

VEGETABLES AND FRUIT
Choose a wide variety

MEAT, FISH AND ALTERNATIVES
Choose lower-fat alternatives whenever you can

BREAD, POTATOES, PASTA AND OTHER CEREALS
Eat all types, and choose high-fibre kinds whenever you can

FATTY AND SUGARY FOO
Try not to eat these too often, and when you do, have small amounts

MILK, CHEESE AND YOGURT
Choose lower-fat alternatives whenever you can

In other words:

- Eat a high proportion of starchy foods such as bread, cereals, potatoes, pasta and rice.
- Eat a high proportion of vegetables and fruit.
- Eat moderate quantities of meat (or alternatives), low-fat milk and dairy produce.
- Carry on enjoying food 'treats' – in small amounts.

History of the healthy plate model

The National Food Guide healthy eating plate model provides the latest advice on healthy eating.

In 1992, the British government published a white paper called *The Health of the Nation*. This aimed to promote public health, rather than concentrating on curing disease, as was the previous approach. Its new strategy was to 'add years to life – and add life to years': to help people to live longer and spend their additional years free from ill health.

HEART DISEASE One of the main aims was to reduce the number of deaths and disabilities from heart disease: that is, both coronary heart disease – the single largest cause of death and main cause of premature death in Britain – and strokes. Because one of the main causes of heart disease is an unbalanced diet that is too high in fat, diet and nutrition targets were set for the year 2005, to reduce the average percentage of food energy (calories) derived from:

• Saturated fats – by at least 35 per cent (to 11 per cent of total food energy/intake).
• Total fat – by at least 12 per cent (to no more than 35 per cent of total food energy/intake).

It was also hoped to reduce the proportion of obese men by at least a quarter, and of obese women by at least a third.

CANCER Although two-thirds of cases of cancer are related to diet, targets for reducing cancer rates through changes in diet were not set because it was felt not enough was known to make specific recommendations. However, balancing your diet according to the healthy plate model should also reduce the risk of diet-related cancers.

Current advice on diet to lower the risk of cancer is to eat less fat, especially saturated fat; to eat more starchy foods, vegetables and fruit (especially those rich in vitamin C and carotenes); to eat only small amounts of salt-cured, salt-pickled and smoked foods; and to drink alcohol in moderation, if at all.

Our complete diet
To achieve the targets set for 2005 it was necessary to take an

holistic approach: that is, to look at the complete diet. Instead of just telling us to cut down on fat, the guidelines recognise that if we are to reduce fat consumption we have to eat other foods to make up the 'lost' calories.

The result is *The National Food Guide* recommendation that we:

• Eat double the current amount of starchy, fibre-rich bread, potatoes, pasta and rice.

• Eat at least five portions of vegetables and fruit each day.

In drawing up *The National Food Guide,* the recommendations of various government reports were followed. These included the COMA (Committee on Medical Aspects of Food Policy) reports on Nutritional Aspects of Cardiovascular Disease, and Dietary Reference Values (the amount of vitamins and minerals we need to be healthy) – see glossary).

The effectiveness of the plate model

The National Food Guide's plate model is the result of the conclusion that: a pictorial selection guide, based on a total diet approach, is the most helpful in providing consumers with a simple, practical and realistic guide for selecting a balanced diet.

Extensive market research showed the plate model to be far more effective in conveying the message of dietary balance than a healthy eating pyramid/triangle, rainbow or kaleidoscope diagram. Consultation with the food industry, health educators, health professionals and the public confirmed the acceptability of the plate model. Work continues on how to develop the project further.

Meanwhile, the aim is to learn from the model how to discriminate between different food groups on the basis of fat, fibre, added sugar and salt content, and how to use that information to select a balanced diet.

CHAPTER 1

Do You Need to Change?

Mae West had the right idea when she said, 'It's not the men in my life, it's the life in my men'. While she may have been thinking of a more direct route to a man's heart than via his stomach, her sentiments are echoed in the main aim of *Healthy Eating on a Plate*.

After all, no one wants to live to be a hundred if they are crippled by the side effects of a lifetime's bad eating and lifestyle, for example, heart disease, strokes and arthritis. But who would not want to live to a ripe old age if they could still enjoy the company of their family and friends, could get around easily and even issue the occasional invitation to 'come up and see me sometime'?

The Healthy Eating on a Plate promise

By making a balanced choice of food, as illustrated on the plate (page 8), you are likely to lose weight if you are overweight, or avoid putting on weight, which helps to:

1 Reduce your risk of heart disease, strokes, some cancers, arthritis and maturity-onset diabetes.
2 Improve your self-confidence, as you will be more in control of your eating habits.
3 Make you less likely to suffer constipation and other discomforts associated with poor diet.

Of course, what your parents and grandparents died of also comes into the equation. If you are genetically prone to any of the above, then in some cases you may not avoid them entirely. Even so, it is still important to take all the self-help measures you can to protect yourself. Changing what you eat is one area of life that is most within your control – along with taking enough exercise and giving up smoking, if you need to.

What do you eat?

Answer the questions below (worked out by the Health Education Authority) to discover how much you eat in terms of portions of different foods each day. The foods are arranged in food groups that correspond to the groupings on the plate model.

Write down how many portions of the foods listed below that you eat *on an average day,* and describe your usual choice of food – not what you think you should be eating, or what you think is the 'right' answer! When you have completed all the sections as fully as possible, turn to Chapter 2 to compare what you eat now with what you should be eating.

How many portions of the following foods do you eat in a normal day?

tbsp = 1 tablespoonful

tsp = 1 teaspoonful

Bread, potatoes, pasta and other cereals
_____ breakfast cereal (3 tbsp)

_____ bread/toast (slices)

_____ pitta bread (small) or chapatti

_____ bread roll, bap or bun

_____ crackers (3)

_____ potatoes (1 medium/175g/6oz or 3 new)

_____ rice, pasta or noodles, cooked (2 tbsp)

_____ plantain, green banana, sweet potato, cooked (2 tbsp)

_____ TOTAL

Vegetables and fruit
_____ vegetables: fresh, frozen or canned (2 tbsp)

_____ salad (small)

_____ fresh fruit: apple, orange etc. See list page 69

_____ stewed or canned fruit (2tbsp)

_____ fruit juice (small glass/3½ fl oz/100ml)

_____ TOTAL

Milk, cheese and yogurt
_____ full-fat milk, gold, silver or
red [homogenised] top (200ml/⅓ pint)

_____ semi-skimmed milk: red-striped top (200ml/⅓pint)

_____ skimmed milk: blue checked top (200ml/⅓ pint)

_____ hard cheese, cheddar-type
(matchbox-sized piece/40g/1½oz)

_____ yogurt, cottage cheese, fromage frais (small pot/120g/4½oz)

_____ TOTAL

Meat, fish and alternatives

_____ beef, pork, ham, lamb, liver, kidney, chicken, oily fish
(a piece the size of a pack of playing cards/50–70g/2–3oz)

_____ white fish (100–150g/4–5oz)

_____ fish fingers (3)

_____ eggs (2)

_____ cheese, cheddar-type (a matchbox-sized piece/40g/1½oz)

_____ baked beans or other cooked pulses, lentils, dhal
(3 tbsp/200g/7oz)

_____ nuts, peanut butter and other nut products (2tbsp/50g/2o

_____ TOTAL

Fats

_____ margarine, butter (1 tsp)

_____ low-fat spread (2 tsp)

_____ cooking oil, fat, ghee (1 tsp)

_____ mayonnaise, vinaigrette or other oily
salad dressing (1 tsp)

_____ TOTAL

Fatty and sugary foods

_____ sugar, eg. in drinks, on cereal (1 tsp)

_____ crisps and equivalents (1 small bag)

_____ pork pie, sausage roll (1 small)

_____ doughnut, Danish pastry

_____ cake, pie (1 slice)

_____ ice-cream (1 scoop)

_____ biscuits (3)

_____ chocolate (1 small bar)

_____ TOTAL

Drinks

_____ coffee (1 cup/mug)
_____ tea (1 cup/mug)
_____ squash, fizzy drinks (1 glass or can)
_____ diet, slimline or sugar-free drinks (1 glass or can)
_____ water (1 glass)
_____ TOTAL

Alcoholic drinks

_____ beer, lager (300ml/½ pint)
_____ wine (1 small glass/120ml/4fl oz)
_____ spirits (pub measure/25ml/1fl oz/⅙ gill)
_____ liqueur, cocktail or other drinks (pub measure/25ml/1fl oz/⅙ gill)
_____ TOTAL

Other foods (composite foods)

Are there any other foods that you eat regularly that have not been mentioned so far? These might include:
• 'Mixed' or 'composite' foods, such as pizza, lasagne or shepherd's pie.
• Traditional foods, such as lassi, paneer, creamed coconut, hummous, taramasalata, baklava.
• New foods, such as Quorn, yogurt drink, very low-fat spread.
If so, list them over page.

Number
of portions   Food

_____ . . . .
_____ . . . .
_____ . . . .
_____ . . . .
_____ . . . .
_____ . . . .
_____ . . . .
_____ . . . .
_____ . . . .
_____ . . . .
_____ . . . .
_____ . . . .
_____ . . . .
_____ . . . .
_____ . . . .
_____ . . . .
_____ . . . .
_____ . . . .
_____ . . . .
_____ . . . .
_____ . . . .
_____ . . . .
_____ . . . .
_____ . . . .
_____ . . . .
_____ . . . .

_____ TOTAL

How do you match up?

What you eat		What you are aiming for per day
TOTAL	FOOD TYPE	IDEAL
_____	Bread, potatoes, pasta and other cereals	5-11 portions
_____	Vegetables and fruit	5 or more
_____	Milk, cheese and yogurt	2-3 lower fat versions
_____	Meat, fish and alternatives	2-3 lower fat versions
_____	Fats	0-3
_____	Fatty and sugary food	1 only
_____	Drinks	6-8
_____	Alcoholic drinks women	up to 14 per week
	men	up to 21 per week
_____	Other foods (composite foods)	No target set

Choosing your food to match the guide

Healthy Eating on a Plate portion goals give the average amounts of foods to select each day for a healthy diet. They add up to the right balance of foods to choose from the four main good groups:

1 Bread, potatoes, pasta and other cereals
2 Vegetables and fruit
3 Milk and dairy foods
4 Meat, fish and alternatives

Plus an allowance for 'extras' such as fats, and fatty and sugary foods

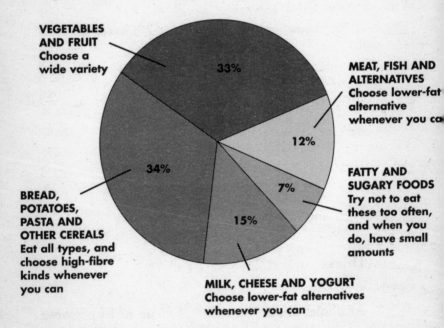

VEGETABLES AND FRUIT
Choose a wide variety — 33%

MEAT, FISH AND ALTERNATIVES
Choose lower-fat alternative whenever you ca — 12%

FATTY AND SUGARY FOODS
Try not to eat these too often, and when you do, have small amounts — 7%

BREAD, POTATOES, PASTA AND OTHER CEREALS
Eat all types, and choose high-fibre kinds whenever you can — 34%

MILK, CHEESE AND YOGURT
Choose lower-fat alternatives whenever you can — 15%

Meeting your needs

All your nutritional needs will be met if you choose foods in these proportions. Each of the main food groups is rich in different nutrients. For example, calcium is available from milk and dairy foods; iron and protein come from meat and alternatives, vitamin C from vegetables and fruit, and the bread, cereal and potato group provide energy (from starch), and fibre.

The balanced choice from the plate model shows that:

- Two-thirds of your food should, ideally, be starchy foods such as bread, cereal, potatoes, plus vegetables and fruit.
- One-third of your food should ideally be low-fat meat (or alternatives) and low-fat dairy produce.
- Fatty and sugary foods should be regarded as treats or 'extras'.

Why are some food 'extras'?

Fats, fatty and sugary foods and drinks, including alcohol, offer only fat, sugar and/or calories. They do not give you the valuable amounts of nutrients (vitamins and minerals) found in foods from the four main food groups. You can obtain all the fat you need from the four main food groups. And, as added sugar (see Chapter 7) is not needed at all in a healthy diet, there is no nutritional reason to eat these 'extras'.

However, as most of us enjoy them, they are included. It would be unrealistic to expect everyone to give up their favourite extras. So, to help you change to a healthier diet, they are included. The art of making a balanced choice is to consume them in moderation.

Everyone is different

While *The National Food Guide* gives the approximate portions of foods needed from each main food group it is important to recognise that everyone has different needs. The number of portions from each food group suitable for you depends on many factors including your age, sex, how active you are and what your weight is.

Only individual consultation with a dietitian, doctor or

nurse will provide a prescription of exactly how much you are likely to need from each food group. Most people do not need this specialist advice, which is probably only necessary for Olympic athletes and others with very specific needs. But it is possible to make more detailed suggestions of what *your* needs may be.

CHAPTER 2

How the Perfect Plateful Measures Up

What *should* you be putting on *your* plate?

Your sex, age and activity level will dictate how many portions of each food group you need to eat. You may find the following suggestions helpful. They are for people who are not overweight (ie, not on a slimming diet).

Size versus frequency

For most people, the recommendations will mean eating more vegetables and fruit and more bread and cereals. There are two ways to do this: eat them more often, or increase the amount you eat. As most people eat only three or four meals a day, it will probably be easiest to increase the number of times a day you eat vegetables and fruit. However, for some groups of men who might be expected to eat up to 11 portions a day of foods such as bread and cereals, it will be easier to increase the size of portions. Men in this extreme group might, for example, eat three or four times the amount of rice they would normally have with a curry, or pile the potatoes onto their plate with a stew or roast meat.

This table gives the portions of food to eat each day. A fuller version starting on page 24 explains in more detail which foods to eat, and why they are needed. Please read both versions.

WOMEN	Bread, potatoes, pasta	Vegetables and fruit	Milk and dairy foods	Meat, fish and alternatives	Fats	Fatty and sugary foods
11-14 active	6-8 a day	At least 5 a day	2-3 a day	About 2 a day	0-3 a day	1 a day (if liked)
11-14 sedentary	5-6 a day					Only occasionally
15-19 active	7-10 a day			3 a day		1 a day (if liked)
15-19 sedentary	6-8 a day			2 a day		Only occasionally
19-49 active	7-10 a day			3 a day		1 a day (if liked)
Pregnancy	10 per cent more from all food groups for the last three months					
Breast feeding	25 per cent more food from all food groups					
19-49 sedentary	6-8 a day	At least 5 a day	2-3 a day	2 a day	0-3 a day	Only occasionally
50-65+	6-8 a day	Aim for 5 a day		2 a day choose oily fish		Only occasionally

This table gives the portions of food to eat each day. A fuller version starting on page 26 explains in more detail which foods to eat, and why they are needed. Please read both versions.

MEN	Bread, potatoes, pasta	Vegetables and fruit	Milk & dairy foods	Meat, fish and alternatives	Fats	Fatty and sugary foods
11-14 active	9-10 a day	At least 5 a day	3 a day	About 2 a day	0 - 3 a day	1-2 a day (if liked)
11-14 sedentary	6-8 a day		2-3 a day			1 a day (if liked)
15-18 active	10-11 a day		3 a day	3 a day		1-2 a day (if liked)
15-18 sedentary	9-10 a day			2 a day		
19-49 active	10-11 a day			3 a day		
19-49 sedentary	9-10 a day			2 a day		
50-65+	7-10 a day		2-3 a day	2-3 a day		1 a day (if liked)
65+	6-8 a day					

Women	Bread, potatoes, pasta and other cereals	Vegetables and fruit	Milk and dairy foods	Meat, fish and alternatives	Fatty and sugary foods
	These food should be the main part of most meals. An example of a portion is a slice of bread or a medium potato	Eat a mixture of different types. An example of a portion is a medium banana or an apple	Choose lower fat versions whenever you can. An example of a portion is a glass of milk, a small pot of yogurt or 2 slices of processed cheese	Eat fish, especially oily fish, at least twice a week. Remove fat from meat or buy low-fat types. An example of a portion is a chicken breast, a medium fillet of fish, or 3 tbsp of cooked beans, peas or lentils	Use low-fat monounsaturated or polyunsaturated spreads. For cooking use polyunsaturated vegetable oil, or olive oil
11–14 Active	These foods provide you with the energy you need to grow and be active. They should be the main part of most meals and snacks, and you would expect to eat about 6–8 portions a day	Aim for at least 5 portions a day. Iron from meat, fish and alternative foods is absorbed better if vegetables and fruit containing vitamin C are eaten at the same time	Calcium is particularly important in building and maintaining bones. 2–3 portions a day should be eaten	Iron is important for preventing anaemia. Vegetarians can obtain iron from foods such as lentils and peas. Eat about 2 portions a day from this group	If you are active a sugary or fatty food once a day will do no harm, but eat sugary foods as part of a meal to reduce the risk of tooth decay
Sedentary	As above. Eat about 5–6 portions a day				Avoid fatty and sugary foods to prevent weight gain

15–18 Active	These foods provide you with the energy you need to grow and be active. They should be the main part of most meals and snacks. Eat about 7–10 portions a day	As 11–14, but eat about 3 portions a day	As above
Sedentary	These foods provide you with the energy you need to grow. Eat about 6–8 portions a day	About 2 portions a day	As above
19–49 Active	These foods provide you with the energy you need to be active. They should be the main part of most meals and snacks, and you should eat about 7–10 portions a day	About 3 portions a day	As above
Sedentary	You need to eat about 6–8 portions a day	About 2 portions a day	As above
50–65+	You need to eat about 6–8 portions a day	About 2 portions a day. Oily fish also contains vitamin D to keep bones strong	Only eat fatty or sugary foods occasionally. Butter and margarine also contain vitamin D

Pregnant

For the last three months of your pregnancy you may need to eat about 10 per cent more food, from all of the food groups

Breastfeeding

While you are breastfeeding to provide all your baby's food you will need to eat about 25 per cent more food, from all of the food groups

Men	Bread, potatoes, pasta and other cereals	Vegetables and fruit	Milk and dairy foods	Meat, fish and alternatives	Fatty and sugary foods
	These foods should be the main part of most meals. An example of a portion is a slice of bread or a medium potato	Eat a mixture of different types. An example of a portion is a medium banana or an apple	Choose lower fat versions whenever you can. An example of a portion is a glass of milk, a small pot of yogurt or 2 slices of processed cheese	Eat fish, especially oily fish, at least twice a week. Remove fat from meat or buy low-fat types. An example of a portion is a chicken breast, a medium fillet of fish, or 3 tbsp of cooked beans, peas or lentils	Use low-fat monounsaturated or polyunsaturated spreads. For cooking use polyunsaturated vegetable oil or olive oil
11–14 Active	These foods provide you with the energy you need to grow and be active. They should be the main part of most meals and snacks, and you would expect to eat about 9–10 portions a day	Aim for at least 5 portions a day	About 3 portions a day	About 3 portions a day. Vegetarians can obtain iron from foods such as lentils and peas, and it is absorbed better if fruits and vegetables containing vitamin C are eaten at the same time	If you are active, a sugary or fatty food once or twice a day will do no harm, but try to eat sugary foods as part of a meal to reduce the risk of tooth decay
Sedentary	These foods provide you with the energy you need to grow. Eat about 6–8 portions a day		About 2–3 portions a day	About 2 portions a day	A sugary or fatty food once a day will do no harm, but try to eat sugary foods as part of a meal to reduce the risk of tooth decay

Age / activity				
15–18 Active	You have very high energy needs at this stage in your life. These foods provide you with the energy you need to grow and be active. They should be the main part of most meals and snacks. Eat about 10–11 portions a day	About 3 portions a day	About 3 portions a day	A sugary or fatty food once or twice a day will do no harm, but try and eat sugary foods as part of a meal to reduce the risk of tooth decay
Sedentary	Eat about 9–10 portions a day			
19–49 Active	These foods provide you with energy. They should be the main part of most meals and snacks. Eat about 10–11 portions a day			
Sedentary	Eat about 9–10 portions a day			
50–65	7–10 portions a day	About 2–3 portions a day	About 2–3 portions a day. Oily fish also contains vitamin D to keep bones strong.	As above. Butter and margarine also contain vitamin D
65+	You would expect to eat 6–8 portions a day			

Babies and Children

For portions for babies and children, turn to Chapter 10, pages 156-7.

Are you active or sedentary?

Exercise is vital for health, from building strong bones in childhood to preventing osteoporosis in old age; and it can do an enormous amount to improve body shape – the aim of most slimmers. In return for doing between three and five 20-minute sessions of aerobic exercise per week (see below) you can lose weight, lower your risk of heart disease, reduce stress and fatigue and improve your body's flexibility.

Aerobic exercise involves exercising at 60 to 80 per cent of your maximum heart rate. To discover your maximum heart rate, subtract your age in years from 220, which gives you the maximum heart rate in beats per minute that is necessary for effective aerobic exercise. Measure your maximum heart rate by taking your pulse at your neck or wrist.

For example, if your age is 35 years, 220 – 35 = 185 beats per minute, maximum heart rate.

60 per cent of 185 = 111 beats per minute

80 per cent of 185 = 148 beats per minute

Therefore, for effective aerobic exercise, a person aged 35 years should increase their heart rate to between 111 and 148 beats per minute.

However, if you are unused to exercise, to start with work to 50 per cent of your maximum capacity (ie, 220 minus your age, x 50 per cent).

Exercise Target Levels for Different Age Groups

Age (men and women)	Target Levels
16–34	Activity Level 5
35–54	Activity Level 4
55–74	Activity Level 3

Activity Level Scale

Activity Level	Number of 20-minute periods during four weeks
5	12 or more periods of vigorous activity
4	12 or more periods of a mix of moderate and vigorous
3	12 or more periods of moderate activity
2	5–11 periods of a mix of moderate and vigorous activity
1	1–4 periods of a mix of moderate and vigorous activity

LIGHT ACTIVITY

- Walking for two miles plus at an average or slow pace.
- Light DIY such as decorating.
- Table tennis, golf, social dancing, bowls, fishing, darts and snooker.
- Exercises that don't make you breathless or sweaty.

MODERATE ACTIVITY

- Long walks over two miles at a brisk or fast pace.
- Football, swimming, tennis, aerobics and cycling if not out of breath or sweaty.
- Table tennis, golf, social dancing and exercises if out of breath or sweaty.
- Heavy DIY (mixing cement), heavy gardening (digging), heavy housework (spring cleaning).

VIGOROUS ACTIVITY

- Hill walking at a brisk pace.
- Squash, running, football, tennis, aerobics and cycling if out of breath or sweaty.
- Some occupations that involve frequent climbing, lifting or carrying heavy loads.

Starting exercise

It's never too late to begin exercise. However, if you have not exercised before, or are over 35, check first with your GP, and have a proper fitness assessment and programme of suitable exercise worked out for you at a local authority class or private club.

Build up gradually to the targets above by first moving up from less strenuous activities until you reach or surpass your age target. Don't try to start at Activity Level 5.

Regular exercise also means you can eat more (but not to excess) without putting on weight. And remember, the more active you are the more calories you burn. Walk rather than take the car or the bus, and climb the stairs rather than take an escalator or lift.

Are you the correct weight?

Body Mass Index is a good indication of whether you are the correct weight.

To work out your BMI:

1 Measure your height in metres and multiply the figure by itself.
2 Measure your weight in kilograms.
3 Divide the weight by the height squared (ie, the result of 1 above)

Check your result against the key on the opposite page.

For example, if your height is 1.6m, and your weight is 75kg: 1.6 x 1.6 = 2.56, 75 divided by 2.56 = 29.3

Therefore, using the table below, your BMI indicates that you are overweight and should lose some weight.

HEIGHT CHART
Imperial heights with approximate metric equivalents

IMPERIAL	METRIC	IMPERIAL	METRIC
4ft 10in	1.47m	5ft 9in	1.75m
4ft 11in	1.50m	5ft 10in	1.78m
5ft	1.52m	5ft 11in	1.80m
5ft 1in	1.55m	6ft	1.83m
5ft 2in	1.57m	6ft 1in	1.85m
5ft 3in	1.60m	6ft 2in	1.88m
5ft 4in	1.62m	6ft 3in	1.90m
5ft 5in	1.65m	6ft 4in	1.93m
5ft 6in	1.67m	6ft 5in	1.95m
5ft 7in	1.70m	6ft 6in	1.98m
5ft 8in	1.73m		

CATEGORY	BMI RANGE
Underweight	Less than 20
Ideal	20–25
Overweight: advisable to lose weight if you are under 50 years old	25–30
Seriously overweight: you should lose weight	30–40
Definitely too fat: lose weight now	More than 40

Your *Healthy Eating on a Plate* Food Goal

Fill in the tables below.

What I eat now Number of portions:					
Bread	Fruit	Milk	Meat	Fats	Fatty/sugary

Healthy Eating on a Plate Food Goal Number of portions:					
Bread	Fruit	Milk	Meat	Fats	Fatty/sugary

What to do next

Don't panic and think that you have to stick rigidly to an exact number of portions each day. Making a balanced choice of foods is about forming long-term healthy eating habits. It won't kill you if you enjoy a meal, or several occasional meals, that contain too much fat and not enough portions of vegetables. Problems arise when unbalanced choices are repeated for long periods. Even then, everyone varies and it is very difficult to say what the effects of any particular diet will have on an individual person's health.

However, it is a good idea to learn how to make balanced choice and to keep to basic eating patterns and habits that are likely to lead to good health. Generally, that involves eating regular meals from a variety of food groups.

The importance of regular meals

Regular meals need not mean that you have to sit down to three 'square' meals a day, at the same time every day. Eating out of habit and not because of hunger can also lead to weight problems. However, formal meals – even for toddlers, who should be seated and possibly wearing a bib – will help prevent the kind of 'grazing' or eating on the hoof that can easily lead to weight problems.

What you need to do is to find your own happy medium. Custom and practice vary among families and cultures and what is convenient for some people may not be for others. Some people eat two larger meals per day and others eat six small or snack meals a day. So long as the meals are well balanced and do not exceed your calorie requirements, either system is fine. The most important thing is to make the balanced choice to meet your needs, ideally on a day-to-day basis, but certainly over a period of weeks and months.

Breakfast is the most important meal of the day because it follows a period of fasting during sleep. For toddlers and young children a sensible breakfast is vital. Lunch is also important, to fuel activities for the rest of the day. An evening meal should be smaller, although many people's working practices dictate that the largest meal is eaten in the evening.

Eating between meals is not a good idea, especially if you eat sweets or chocolates, biscuits or cakes, because this reduces the appetite for vegetables, fruit, cereals and protein foods at the next main meal. See Chapter 8 for ideas for healthier snacks.

What is a portion?

If, after seeing how many portions are recommended, you do not want to increase the number of times when you eat particular foods, remember that you can just serve larger portions to meet your *Healthy Eating on a Plate* Food Goal.

Bread, potatoes, pasta and other cereals

- Eat 5–11 portions daily.
- Eat all types and choose high fibre varieties whenever you can.

One portion equals:
3 tbsp breakfast cereal
1 slice bread or toast
1 bread roll, bap or bun
1 small pitta bread or chapatti
3 crackers or crispbreads
1 medium (175g/6oz) potato or 3 new potatoes
2 tbsp cooked rice, pasta or noodles
2 tbsp cooked plantain, green banana or sweet potato

BREAD – QUICK YES/NO QUIZ

1 Do you usually eat bread and breakfast cereals that are high in fibre? Yes . . . .   No . . . .
2 Do you eat 4–6 slices of (wholemeal) bread most days? Yes . . . .   No . . . .
3 Do you eat potatoes, pasta or rice at least once a day? Yes . . . .   No . . . .
4 Do you eat beans, lentils or other pulses more than once a week? Yes . . . .   No . . . .

Answers page 41.

The Benefits of Bread
Starchy carbohydrates are the best food source of energy. They also contain B vitamins for healthy nerves and digestion, and fibre for avoiding constipation and lowering blood cholesterol.

Vegetables and fruit

- Eat 5–9 portions daily.
- Choose a wide variety.

One portion equals:
2 tbsp vegetables (cooked or raw). See list on page 71.
1 small salad
1 piece fresh fruit
2 tbsp stewed or canned fruit
1 small (100ml/3½fl oz) fruit juice

VEGETABLES AND FRUIT - QUICK YES/NO QUIZ

1 Do you regularly eat vegetables (in addition to potatoes) with meat/fish/vegetarian alternatives?
Yes . . . .   No . . . .
2 Do you regularly eat two or more vegetables (in addition to potatoes) with meat/fish/vegetarian alternatives?
Yes . . . .   No . . . .
3 Do you eat salad as a main meal more than once or twice a week? Yes . . . .   No . . . .
4 Do you eat vegetables with readymeals and takeaways?
Yes . . . .   No . . . .
5 Do you eat fruit (fresh, frozen, canned or dried) each day? Yes . . . .   No . . . .
Answers on page 41.

The Benefits of Vegetables and Fruit
Vegetables and fruits are the best source of vitamin C for immunity and wound healing. They also contain carotenes for antioxidant protection against heart disease and cancer; folates for prevention of anaemia and antioxidant action (folic acid before and during pregnancy to prevent spina bifida) and fibre.

Milk, cheese and yogurt

- Eat 2–3 portions daily.
- Choose low-fat alternatives.

One portion equals:
200ml/⅓ pint full-fat milk (gold, silver or red [homogenised] top)
200ml/⅓ pint semi-skimmed milk (red striped top)
200ml/⅓ pint skimmed milk (blue checked top)
Matchbox-sized piece/40g/1½oz cheddar-type cheese
Small pot/120g/4½oz yogurt, cottage cheese or fromage frais

MILK – QUICK YES/NO QUIZ

1 Do you eat full-fat cheese less than twice a week?
  Yes .... No ....
2 Do you choose low-fat yogurts? Yes .... No ....
3 Do you use skimmed milk? Yes .... No ....
4 Do you eat cream or cream-based cakes or puddings
  less than three times a week?
  Yes .... No ....
5 Do you choose cottage cheese or fromage frais
  or medium-fat cheese such as Edam?
  Yes .... No ....

Answers page 41.

The Benefits of Milk

Dairy foods are the best source of calcium for strong bones, teeth and nerves. They also provide some protein for growth and repair; vitamin B12 to prevent anaemia and vitamins A and D for healthy eyes and bones. Dairy foods are especially important for babies and young children.

Meat, fish and alternatives

- Eat 2-3 portions daily.
- Choose lower fat alternatives.

One portion equals:
50–70g/2–3oz (the size of a pack of playing cards) beef, pork, ham, lamb, liver, kidney, chicken or oily fish.
100–150g/4–5oz white fish (not fried in batter)
3 fish fingers
2 eggs (eat up to 4 a week)
Matchbox-sized piece/40g/1½oz cheddar-type cheese
3 tbsp/200g/7oz baked beans or other cooked pulses, lentils
2 tbsp/50g/2oz nuts, peanut butter or other nut products

MEAT – QUICK YES/NO QUIZ

1 Do you have at least one meat-free day a week?
  Yes . . . .   No . . . .
2 Do you eat sausages, meat pies, burgers less than twice a week? Yes . . . .   No . . . .
3 Do you eat fish (not including fried) twice a week?
  Yes . . . .   No . . . .
4 Do you cut the visible fat off meat and remove the skin from poultry before eating it?   Yes . . . .   No . . . .
5 Do you eat meals based on beans, pulses or lentils more than twice a week?   Yes . . . .   No . . . .

Answers page 41.

The Benefits of Protein Foods
These foods provide iron which prevents anaemia; protein for growth and repair; B vitamins for healthy nerves and digestion, especially B12 for preventing anaemia; minerals zinc and magnesium for growth, healthy bones, skin and other functions.

Fats

- Limit to 3 portions daily.

One portion equals:
1 tsp margarine or butter
2 tsp low-fat spread
1 tsp cooking oil, fat or ghee
1 tsp mayonnaise, vinaigrette or other oily salad dressing

FATS – QUICK YES/NO QUIZ

1 Do you use a low-fat spread rather than butter or margarine?   Yes . . . .   No . . . .
2 Do you eat bread and crackers without spreading fat on them, especially with cheese?   Yes . . . .   No . . . .
3 Do you choose a cooking oil that is high in unsaturated fats?   Yes . . . .   No . . . .
4 Do you serve vegetables without butter or margarine? Yes . . . .   No . . . .
5 Do you serve salads with the dressing on the side? Yes . . . .   No . . . .

Answers on page 41.

The Benefits of Fats

Fats supply mainly calories, plus some vitamin A and D needed particularly by babies and young children for growth. Vegetable fats also provide essential fatty acids and vitamin E. Animal fats provide mainly saturated fat, so the nutrients they provide are better supplied by other foods.

Fatty and sugary foods

- Limit to one per day.

These include:

Cream (and cream-based desserts and toppings), chocolate and chocolate spreads, crisps, biscuits, Danish pastries, doughnuts, cake, ice-cream, jellies, rich sauces, fatty gravies, snack foods (such as Bombay mix and other savouries), soft drinks, sweets, sugar (in drinks, on cereals, in cakes etc), sugar confectionery, sausages, fatty bacon. (Pork pies, meat pies and pasties are considered composite items; pâtés and luncheon meat are considered to be meats.)

FATTY AND SUGARY FOODS – QUICK YES/NO QUIZ

1 Do you eat take-away foods less than twice a week?
Yes .... No ....
2 Do you eat crisps less than three times a week?
Yes .... No ....
3 Do you eat chocolate or equivalent less than once week?
Yes .... No ....
4 Do you eat two, or fewer, biscuits a day?
Yes .... No ....
5 Do you eat desserts at only one meal a day, or on fewer occasions? Yes .... No ....
Answers on page 41.

Answers on page 41.

Disadvantages of Fatty and Sugary Foods
Fatty and sugary foods provide very few nutrients and lots of fat, sugar and sometimes salt. The few vitamins and minerals they provide are supplied in larger quantities for fewer calories by other foods in the four main food groups.

Other Foods

Under this heading you may have listed several so-called composite or mixed foods. These have not been dealt with by *The National Food Guide* in its plate model.

Examples of composite foods are recipe dishes such as beef stew, steak and kidney pudding, hot pot, Irish stew, pizza, casseroles, lasagne, sandwiches; ethnic dishes such as bhajis, pakoras, speciality Chinese/Indian pastries, flans and quiches, moussaka, spaghetti bolognese. Plus puddings such as bread and butter pudding, treacle tart, and so on.

Several other foods are also missing from *The National Food Guide*. These include alcohol, baby foods, baking aids, chutneys and condiments such as ketchup, herbs, spices and seeds, instant coffee, tea and bedtime drinks.

The healthy way to include composite foods in your diet is to identify the main food item or ingredient in the composite food and then add other foods from different groups to build a balanced meal. For example: a ham, cheese and mushroom pizza contains a dough base (from the bread, potato and cereals group); cheese (from the milk and dairy group), ham (from the meat, fish and alternatives group). The proportion of vegetables (ie, mushroom and tomato) relative to the other ingredients is small, compared with the amount of vegetables and fruit on the *Healthy Eating on a Plate* model. So add a mixed salad or cooked vegetables, and eat a piece of fresh fruit for dessert to balance the meal and/or a drink of fruit juice.

Treat recipe dishes or ready-made meals in the same way as composite foods. Always serve additional vegetables (fresh, frozen or canned) with ready meals. And add portions of carbohydrate foods too, such as additional rice, potatoes, bread or naan bread.

Practical help to eat healthily

For many of us it is not easy today to eat healthily because we are surrounded by easily available food – especially fatty and sugary snacks. In evolutionary terms we are programmed to take available food when it presents itself, because back in our dim and distant past (and even in living memory during two world wars) we were often not sure where the next meal was coming from. So, it takes some adjustment not to eat food when it is presented.

Some people will not find this a problem. Armed with the information in *Healthy Eating on a Plate*, they will be able to buy and eat what is best for their health. Other people will find it a more difficult. If you think you are in the second group then it is very important to get all the help you can. Practical steps include planning ahead by making shopping lists and sticking to them. You also need to ask family and friends to support your efforts.

You'll find the practical help, advice and tips you need in Chapter 11, The Winning Formula.

Quick Yes/No Quiz Answers
- If the answer to all these questions is yes then you are doing well. Keep it up.
- If you answered yes to three or four in each section that's still very good, but you could do a little more.
- If you answered yes to only one or two you have made a good start. Press on and make a few more changes.
- If you answered no to all the questions, it really is time for you to make some changes.

CHAPTER 3

Step One: Bread, Cereals and Potatoes

Bread, cereals and potatoes are starchy foods and most of us need to double the amount of starchy foods we eat every day. Check your own *Healthy Eating on a Plate* Food Goal on page 32.

Contrary to popular belief, starchy foods are not fattening. They are much lower in calories than fatty and sugary foods and they are also more 'nutrient dense'. That means they contain more vitamins and minerals than fatty and sugary foods which are higher in calories. And because they are rich in fibre, they also fill you up for fewer calories. Eating lots of these foods means you are less likely to suffer from constipation – and you don't have to sprinkle unpalatable bran on your food.

Two key ways to eat more bread, cereal and potatoes
As most of us already eat these foods quite frequently, the best way of increasing the amount we eat is to
1 Make the portions bigger.
2 Make bread, cereal and potatoes the main part of most meals.

What are starchy foods/carbohydrates?

There are two main types of carbohydrate.

1 Starchy foods

Cereals, bread, pasta, potatoes, pulses, whole grains, vegetables and fruit such as root vegetables, sweet potatoes, cassava and plantain all contain fibre, vitamins and minerals. These are the carbohydrates that you need to eat more of to help weight control and prevent heart disease and some cancers.

2 Sugary foods

The scientific name for sugar, whether it is stirred into drinks or eaten in cakes, biscuits, pastries and processed foods is 'extrinsic' or free sugars, so named because they are not an integral part of a food, but refined from the food. As well as sugar, this 'undesirable' type of carbohydrate includes glucose syrup, honey, concentrated fruit juices, and all the synonyms (other names) for sugar that crop up on food labels. This is the type of carbohydrate that we should be eating less of.

Which foods are included as breads, other cereals and potatoes?

Breads - some examples

All types of bread made with and without yeast, including: bannocks, brown rolls, brown bread, chapattis, crispbread, crumpets, fruit buns (currant, raisin, sultana, apricot breads), currant buns, English muffins, Granary bread, burger buns, hot cross buns, malt bread, matzos, milk bread, morning rolls, bran muffins, naan bread, oatcakes, poppadoms, pitta bread, pumpernickel, rye bread, scones (white, wholemeal, potato, fruit, plain, cheese), soda bread, teacakes (fruit), tortillas made with wheat flour, water biscuits, wheatgerm bread, white bread and rolls, wholemeal bread and rolls, wholemeal crackers.

Whenever possible, eat without added fat such as butter or margarine.

Other cereals - some examples

Barley (wholegrain and pearl), Bemax, breakfast cereals, brown rice, buckwheat, bulgar wheat, chapatti flour (white and brown), chick-pea flour, hominy, pasta (all colours and wholemeal), millet flour, noodles (rice, plain, egg), paratha, popcorn, puris, quinoa, rice (all types), rice flour, sago, semolina, soya flour, tapioca, taro, vermicelli, wheat flour (white, brown, wholemeal), wheatgerm.

But *not* fried, extruded snack foods.

Potatoes and starchy staples - some examples

Cassava, plantain, potato waffles, potato flour, instant potato, potatoes, sweet potatoes, yam.

But *not* snack foods such as crisps and other extruded savoury potato snacks.

Ways to eat more bread, cereal and potatoes

For variety and enjoyment, try the following:
• Experiment with different varieties of potatoes: eg, small waxy potatoes for salads, floury varieties for mashing and firm fleshed varieties for boiling.
• Use different types of rice for different dishes: eg, brown as a regular main meal accompaniment, a mixture of wild rice and brown rice for special occasions, arborio rice for risottos, short-grain rice for puddings.
• Use any left-over (cold, cooked) rice in salads, or to mix

with vegetables, fish or meat for stuffed vegetables, such as cabbage leaves, vine leaves, peppers, aubergines.

• Eat the skins on boiled and baked potatoes.

• Replace cakes and biscuits with lower fat items such as wholemeal hot cross buns, wholemeal fruit buns or wholemeal scones. Use minimal amount of spread, if any: for example, 7g/¼oz polyunsaturate spread or 15g/½oz low-fat spread.

• Replace fatty and sugary foods (see Chapter 8, page 144) with other foods from this group.

• Make polenta or cornbread (both made with maize or cornmeal) as accompaniments to suitable dishes.

• Try other cereals such a cracked wheat, bulghur and couscous, eg in taboulleh (cracked wheat salad), falafel (baked, not fried vegetarian 'meatballs'), couscous (grain served with a meat or vegetable stew).

• Sandwiches: no need to use a spread if the bread is fresh, the filling is moist (for example, if they contain lots of salad or grated vegetables), and the sandwiches are not made too far ahead of eating.

• Toasted sandwiches: as above.

• Smorgasbord/open sandwiches: use wholegrain and sourdough rye breads. Top with plenty of salad and a little lean ham or a few prawns (no mayonnaise).

• Bruschetta: Italian ciabatta/focaccia bread spread with olive oil and garlic and topped with wafer-thin ham and Mediterranean vegetables.

• Eat pasta regularly as a main meal. It goes with a myriad of low-fat vegetarian, fish, seafood and meat sauces.

• Use any left-over (cold cooked) pasta in salads.

Types to choose

• Try to eat wholemeal, wholegrain, brown or high fibre

Buying sandwiches

If you are short of time and are buying a ready-made sandwich remember...

• choose those labelled 'low in calories' (usually up to 300 calories) or those marked 'no mayonnaise' because they will be lower in fat.

• Whenever possible, ask for wholemeal bread and don't be afraid to speak up in sandwich bars where the sandwiches are made up as you order them, and say 'No spread!' if low-fat spread is not available.

• Ask for lots of salad filling and avoid tuna, chicken and prawns if they are swimming in mayonnaise.

varieties of bread, breakfast cereal, pasta and rice whenever possible. This is because the grains are 'whole': ie, they have not had the bran or vitamins and minerals refined out of them.

• If you do not like wholemeal bread, try to find another type of high-fibre bread for regular use.

• Eat white bread if you really don't like 'brown' breads, but make sure you eat some other wholegrain cereals (eg, breakfast cereals or brown rice/pasta).

• Try to choose breakfast cereals that do not contain added sugar. For example, Shredded Wheat or Puffed Wheat. Others that contain the whole grain are also good, eg Weetabix. Sugary cereals can still be enjoyed as occasional treats.

• Porridge, made with skimmed milk (full fat up to age two, semi-skimmed to age five) and/or water is an excellent breakfast cereal as the naturally occurring bran in the outer layer of the grain is not removed during processing. Oats are also rich in vitamins and minerals, soluble fibre and protein.

- Use porridge oats to make your own muesli if you are unable to find a brand of no-added sugar muesli that you like. Mix the oats with chopped nuts and dried fruit, plus wheatgerm, if you like it. Either soak overnight in milk or apple juice in the fridge and just before serving grate in some fresh fruit (apple/pear), or slice in a banana, or stir in some berries when in season.
- Make regular use of pasta, including wholewheat.
- Make regular use of rice, especially brown rice.
- Boil or steam noodles, rather than frying.
- Choose lower-fat sauces for pasta and noodles.

Healthier cooking with potatoes

- Boil and steam, or microwave in the minimum amount of water for everyday cooking.
- There's no need to add fat during cooking or at the table, but if you do, use the minimum.
- Moisten jacket (baked) potatoes with either low-fat yogurt, cottage cheese, fromage frais or lower-fat crème fraîche flavoured with chopped fresh herbs (eg parsley, basil, coriander, chervil, fennel, dill) or spices of your choice.
- Mash potatoes by adding skimmed milk and/or low-fat spread and seasoning or herbs (as above) instead of butter/margarine and salt.

Time saver

A pressure cooker can help cut cooking time. It can cook brown rice in 7 minutes and potatoes in 6 minutes. The quicker the food is ready, the less time there is for nibbling on snacks such as crisps. However, if hunger is getting the better of you, nibble on a breadstick (grissini), or a crispbread, rice cakes and rice crackers.

Potato chips
Choose oven chips if buying ready-made ones.
If you make your own, cut them thick and straight to
reduce the amount of fat they soak up. Fry them in a
vegetable oil high in unsaturates such as sunflower,
soya, rapeseed or olive oil. Make sure the oil is hot
enough (at least 170°C/340°F) before frying, but not
hotter or giving off blue smoke.
Use oil for deep frying only once, if possible, but
certainly not more than six times.
Drain chips on absorbent kitchen paper.

• Cook rosti, a Swiss dish of grated and fried potato cakes
with the minimum vegetable oil in a non-stick pan.
• Use mashed potato as a topping for 'pies' instead of
pastry (as it's much lower in fat).
• Make potato salad with low-fat yogurt, cottage cheese,
fromage frais or lower-fat crème fraîche (as above) instead
of mayonnaise.

Occasional use only!

Potatoes Chips and French fries, roast potatoes, sautéed
(fried) potatoes and other high-fat potato dishes, eg potatoes
dauphinoise, potatoes Anna, adding too much butter or
margarine to jacket (baked) potatoes, deep-fried potato skins.

Bread Fried bread, adding too much butter or margarine to
bread and toast, garlic bread.

Rice Fried rice and noodles.

How to eat more starchy foods

BEFORE			AFTER
BREAKFAST	fat	fat	BREAKFAST
Slice of white toast,	9g	5.5g	1 Weetabix, 1 slice
butter and marmalade	cals	cals	wholemeal toast
	195	250	
SNACK	fat	fat	SNACK
2 chocolate biscuits	7g	4.5g	1 wholemeal fruit bun
	cals	cals	
	135	175	
LUNCH	fat	fat	LUNCH
1 round (2 slices) white	15g	7g	2 rounds (4 slices)
bread beef and	cals	cals	wholemeal egg
horseradish sandwich	400	245	salad sandwiches
SNACK	fat	fat	SNACK
1 chocolate cup cake	2g	1g	1 wholemeal muffin
	cals	cals	
	135	125	
DINNER	fat	fat	DINNER
1 fried pork chop,	55g	19g	1 grilled pork escalope,
sautéed potatoes, peas	cals	cals	boiled potatoes, peas,
	955	515	cabbage
DESSERT	fat	fat	DESSERT
Golden syrup sponge	14g	0	Fresh fruit salad
pudding	cals	cals	
	400	80	
TOTAL	fat	fat	**TOTAL**
	102	**37**	
	cals	cals	
	2220	**1390**	

BEFORE				AFTER
BREAKFAST 1 fried egg on 1 slice fried bread	fat 7.5g cals 295	fat 6g cals 150		BREAKFAST 1 poached egg on 1 slice wholemeal toast
SNACK 1 flapjack	fat 6g cals 125	fat 2g cals 90		SNACK 2 ginger nut biscuits
LUNCH 6 fried fish fingers with 2 fried tomatoes, white roll and butter	fat 50g cals 570	fat 13.5g cals 545		LUNCH 6 grilled fish fingers with peas, sweet corn and wholemeal roll
SNACK Mars bar, standard size	fat 12 cals 286	fat 0 cals 76		SNACK 1 banana
DINNER 2 onion bhajis; chicken tikka masala, special fried rice	fat 63g cals 1394	fat 20.5g cals 944		DINNER 2 chapattis; chicken tikka biryani, 1 pilau rice
TOTAL	fat **138.5g** cals **2670**	fat **42** cals **1805**		**TOTAL**

Starchy Recipes

If you tend to plan your meals around meat (or fish, or a vegetarian alternative) take a look at the recipes that follow for ideas to make starchy foods the centre of attention. Then, next time you plan a meal base it on either bread, potatoes, pasta, rice or another cereal.

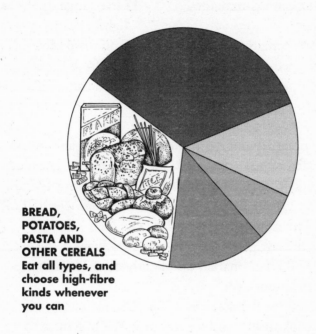

BREAD, POTATOES, PASTA AND OTHER CEREALS
Eat all types, and choose high-fibre kinds whenever you can

Potato Gnocchi in Tomato Sauce

Serves 4

Tomato Sauce
15ml/1tbsp olive oil
1 medium onion, chopped
1 clove garlic, crushed
400g/14oz canned tomatoes,
  chopped
15ml/1tbsp tomato purée
1tbsp chopped fresh basil
1tbsp chopped fresh parsley
Freshly ground black pepper

Gnocchi
700g/1½lb potatoes,
  peeled
100g/4oz plain flour
½ free-range eggs,
  lightly beaten
15ml/1tbsp olive oil
2tbsp freshly grated
  Parmesan cheese

1 Boil the potatoes and mash them, adding salt and pepper.
Turn out onto a floured board. Make a well in the centre and
quickly work in a small amount of the flour, egg and oil,
using a fork. Gradually add the rest of the flour, egg and oil
to make a firm dough.
2 Leave in the refrigerator for 20 minutes. Preheat the oven
to 190°C/375°F/Gas mark 5 and lightly oil a 22cm/9in-
diameter ovenproof dish.
3 Heat the oil for the sauce in a pan. Add the onion and
garlic and cook until translucent. Stir in the tomatoes,
tomato purée and herbs, cover and cook for 15 minutes.
4 Roll the gnocchi dough into a long sausage. Bring a large
pan of salted water to the boil. Cut the dough into
2.5cm/1in lengths, roll them into egg shapes and pop them
into the water to poach for five minutes. They should float
to the top when cooked. Remove with a slotted spoon and
place in the serving dish.
5 Pour over the tomato sauce, sprinkle on the Parmesan
and heat through in the preheated oven.

Double Potato Shepherd's Pie

Serves 4

900g/2lb potatoes
450g/1lb fresh lamb mince or cold roast lamb, diced
1 onion, diced
15ml/1tbsp vegetable oil
2 carrots, grated
1tbsp plain flour
15ml/1tbsp tomato purée
1tsp chopped fresh thyme
300ml/½ pint meat stock
Salt and freshly ground black pepper

1 Boil half the potatoes, drain and mash without adding any fat. Slice the other half into rounds.
2 Preheat the oven to 190°C/375°F/Gas mark 5. Lightly oil a 1.5 litre/2½ pint ovenproof dish.
3 Sauté the onion in the oil until it softens. Add the carrots and lamb and cook, stirring well, for a further five minutes. Pour off any excess fat (only necessary if using fresh mince) and stir in the flour, tomato purée, thyme and stock. Cook for a further 10 minutes until the mixture has thickened. Remove from the heat.
4 Place the sliced potato in the base of the dish and pour on the meat sauce. Top with the mashed potato and bake for 40 minutes until the topping is golden brown.

Chicken and Mushroom Risotto

Serves 4

20g/¾oz dried mushrooms, such as porcini, morelles,
cèpes, champignons
100g/4oz fresh mushrooms such as chestnut,
  pieds de Monton, hedgehog
30ml/2 tbsp olive oil
2 cloves garlic, crushed
1 large onion, chopped
1 stick celery, chopped
450g/1lb chicken, shredded
225g/8oz risotto/Italian arborio rice
Pinch saffron strands
600ml/1 pint vegetable bouillon or chicken stock
25g/1oz freshly grated Parmesan cheese

1 Soak the mushrooms according to the pack instructions
(usually a minimum of 15 minutes in very hot water).
2 Heat the oil in a large, heavy based, 20cm/8in saucepan
and sauté the garlic, onion, and celery for about 5 minutes,
until softened.
3 Stir in the chicken and rice and cook for 5 minutes,
stirring continuously to prevent sticking. Add the saffron
and the mushrooms, including their soaking water (but be
careful not to add any grit that has fallen to the bottom of
the basin during soaking).
4 Stir in some of the stock and simmer for about 20
minutes. Stir occasionally, adding more stock until the rice
has absorbed the stock and is cooked.
5 Stir in the Parmesan, and serve.

Salmon Kedgeree

Serves 4

450g/1lb salmon tailpiece
15ml/1 tbsp vegetable oil
½ tsp ground cinnamon
5 green cardamom pods, bruised
175g/6oz basmati rice, washed
½ tsp turmeric powder
450–600ml/¾–1 pint water or fish stock
25g/1oz flaked almonds, toasted
3 free-range eggs, hard-boiled
Coriander, or flathead parsley leaves, to garnish

1 Poach the salmon in enough water to almost cover for 10 minutes. Remove from the water and cool. Remove the skin and bones and flake the fish. Cover and place on one side.

2 Heat the oil, add the cinnamon and cardamom and fry for a couple of minutes. Stir in the rice and cook until golden. Add the turmeric and the water/fish stock and stir well. Cover the pan and cook on a very low flame for 15 minutes.

3 Add the salmon and continue cooking until the liquid has been absorbed and the rice is cooked – about another 10 minutes.

4 Remove from the heat and stir in the almonds. Garnish with slices of egg and coriander leaves, and serve at once.

Pasta with Vegetables

Serves 4 as a light meal

300ml/½ pint vegetable stock
1 head Romanesco (flowering cauliflower), cut into pieces
2 courgettes, sliced
1 red pepper, de-seeded and sliced
225g/8oz baby carrots, scraped
175g/6oz French beans, trimmed
4 sun-dried tomatoes, sliced
400g/14oz can cannellini or other white beans
75g/3oz pasta shapes
2 tbsp pesto
Parmesan cheese, freshly grated

1 Heat the stock while you prepare the vegetables. Add them (except the tomatoes) to the hot stock, cover and simmer for 10 minutes.
2 Add the tomatoes, beans and continue to cook, uncovered, for a further 10 minutes.
3 In another pan, boil the pasta in plenty of water for about 12–15 minutes until it is cooked but still al dente.
4 Remove from the heat. Stir in the pesto and vegetables and serve with the Parmesan.

Seafood Pasta Sauce

Serves 4

2 garlic cloves, crushed
1 large onion, chopped
2 green peppers, de-seeded and chopped
30ml/2tbsp olive oil
450g/1lb tomatoes, chopped
225g/8oz mussels, cooked
225g/8oz shelled, cooked prawns, defrosted if necessary
50g/2oz anchovies, drained
1 tbsp capers
1 carrot, peeled and grated
225g/8oz spaghetti
Parmesan cheese, freshly grated

1 Gently fry the garlic, onion and peppers in the oil until softened but not browned. Add the tomatoes and cook for about 15 minutes, stirring occasionally, until a thick sauce has formed.
2 Stir in the mussels, prawns, anchovies and capers and heat through.
3 Meanwhile, cook the spaghetti in plenty of salted boiling water until cooked but still *al dente* (offering some resistance when bitten).
4 Just before serving, stir the carrot into the sauce, leaving it crunchy in texture. Toss the sauce and pasta together.

Seafood Lasagne

Serves 4

175g/6oz no pre-cooking required green or white fresh
lasagne
25g/1oz unbleached plain flour
25g/1oz butter or soft margarine
450ml/¾ pint skimmed milk
3 plaice fillets, sliced
60ml/2 tbsp chopped fresh parsley
8 scallops, shelled
2 garlic cloves, crushed
60ml/2 tbsp olive oil
400g/14oz can of tomatoes, roughly chopped
sea salt and freshly ground black pepper

1 Preheat the oven to 190°C/375°F/Gas/Mark 5. Melt the
butter and flour to make a roux and gradually stir in the
milk to make a smooth sauce.
2 Stir in the parsley and plaice. Place half the sauce in the
base of a lightly oiled 20cm (8 inch) square oven-proof
dish. Cover with a layer of lasagne sheets.
3 Gently fry the garlic in the oil and stir in the scallops and
tomatoes. Continue to cook for 5 minutes. Place half the
scallop sauce on top of the pasta.
4 Repeat the layering twice. End with white sauce on top.
Cover the dish with foil and bake for 25 minutes. Remove
the foil for 10 minutes at the end of cooking to lightly
brown the top.

Minestrone

Serves 4

30 ml/2 tbsp olive oil
1 large onion, diced
2 garlic cloves, crushed
2 carrots, diced
2 sticks celery, chopped
100g/4oz French beans, sliced
2 courgettes, sliced
450g/1lb tomatoes, chopped, or 425g/14oz canned
    tomatoes
1.2 litres/2 pints chicken or vegetable stock
2 tsp fresh thyme leaves
400g/14oz can cannellini or other white beans
50g/2oz macaroni, or other pasta for soup
4 tbsp chopped fresh parsley
Salt and freshly ground black pepper
Parmesan cheese, freshly grated

1 Heat the oil in a large saucepan, add the onion and garlic and cook until they begin to soften. Add the remaining vegetables up to and including the tomatoes. Stir well.
2 When all the vegetables have been added, pour in the stock. Bring to the boil, cover and simmer for about 25 minutes.
3 Drain and rinse the beans (if canned), then stir them in, together with the pasta, parsley and seasoning. Simmer for a further 15 minutes, until all the vegetables are tender and the pasta is just cooked.

Polenta 'Pizza'

Serves 2 (as a main course)

Pizza base
150g/5oz polenta or yellow cornmeal
250ml/8fl oz cold water
450ml/15fl oz chicken stock
90ml/6 tbsp Parmesan cheese, grated

Topping
30ml/2 tbsp tomato purée
1 garlic clove, crushed
10ml/2 tsp olive oil
2 tbsp chopped fresh basil
2 ripe tomatoes, sliced thinly
1 tbsp capers
4 artichoke hearts (canned or in oil), sliced
150g/5oz buffalo mozzarella, thinly sliced

1 Blend the polenta and water in a bowl, using a fork.
2 Bring the stock to the boil in a saucepan and add the polenta mixture to it in one go. Stir until the mixture boils and thickens. Reduce the heat, and cook for 10 minutes, stirring all the time to prevent sticking.
3 Remove from the heat and stir in the cheese. Spoon into a lightly oiled 25cm/10in-diameter pizza dish (or cake tin) and smooth the top. Leave to set until cold.
4 Preheat the oven to 190°C/375°F/Gas mark 5. Mix together the tomato purée, garlic, basil and olive oil and spread over the polenta base. Arrange the tomatoes, capers, artichoke hearts and mozzarella on top and bake for 10–15 minutes, until the cheese has melted.

Fruity Bread and Butter Pudding

Serves 6

4 slices bread, 2 white and 2 wholemeal, crusts removed
25g/1 oz butter
75g/3 oz mixed currants and raisins
4 dried apricots, chopped
2 free-range egg yolks
1 free-range egg
40g/1½oz muscovado sugar
½ tsp ground cinnamon
450ml/15fl oz milk
½ tsp vanilla extract (not essence)

1 Preheat the oven to 190°C/375°F/Gas mark 5. Spread the bread with the butter, cut into halves or quarters and arrange in an ovenproof dish, buttered side up.
2 Sprinkle the fruit over the top, pushing some down between and beneath the slices of bread.
3 Whisk the egg yolks, egg, sugar, cinnamon, milk and vanilla extract in a bowl and pour over the bread in the dish. Leave to stand for half an hour.
4 Place the pudding in a bain-marie (roasting pan of hot water) and bake for about 40 minutes until the top is golden brown and the custard set.

NB Using a bain-marie ensures a smooth, uncurdled custard, but you can take a chance and cook the pudding without.

Cheese and Olive Muffins

Serves 4

100g/4oz cornmeal (maize or polenta flour)
100g/4oz wholemeal flour
2 tsp baking powder
225ml/8fl oz buttermilk
60ml/2tbsp olive oil
1 free-range egg, lightly beaten
100g/4oz olives and chopped feta cheese salad
75g/3oz cheddar cheese, grated

1 Mix the flours and baking powder. Stir in the buttermilk, olive oil and egg.
2 Fold in the olives and feta salad and 2oz of the grated cheese.
3 Preheat the oven to 200°C/400°F/Gas 6. Spoon into muffin paper cases placed in a muffin (bun) tray. Bake for 10 min. Quickly and carefully remove from the oven, sprinkle the remaining grated cheese on top and return to the oven for a further 10 min or until an inserted skewer comes out clean.

Apricot Scones

Makes 8

225g/8oz wholemeal flour, or half and half wholemeal
  and unbleached white
5ml/1tsp baking powder
50g/2oz polyunsaturate margarine
50g/2oz demerara sugar
100g/4oz dried apricots, chopped
150ml/5fl oz skimmed milk
10ml/2tsp lemon juice
milk to glaze

1 Preheat the oven to 200°C/400°F/Gas 6.
2 Sift the flour and baking powder into a mixing bowl,
returning the bran from the sieve to the bowl.
3 Rub in the fat. Stir in the sugar and fruit.
4 Add the lemon juice to the milk to sour it and pour onto
the flour. Mix to a soft dough and roll out on a lightly
floured board.
5 Using a 8cm/3in cutter, cut out the scones and place
them on a lightly oiled baking sheet. Glaze with milk and
bake for 15 minutes.

Lunch Box Fruit Cake

Cuts into 8 slices

100g/4oz polyunsaturate margarine
50g/2oz light muscovado sugar
50g/2oz molasses or black treacle
2 free-range eggs
175g/6oz plain flour, half unbleached white and half
   wholemeal
5ml/1 tsp baking powder
50g/2oz currants
50g/2oz raisins

1 Preheat the oven to 190°C/375°F/Gas 5. Lightly oil a
20cm/8in cake tin.
2 Cream the fat, sugar and molasses. Beat in the eggs.
3 Fold in the sifted flour and baking powder. Stir in the
fruit.
4 Spoon the mixture into the prepared tin and bake for 25
minutes or until an inserted skewer comes out clean. Place
a double thickness of greaseproof paper over the top of the
cake for the last 5-10 minutes to prevent over-browning.

CHAPTER 4

Step Two: Vegetables and Fruit

Most of us need to double the amount of vegetables and fruit we eat at present to about 400g/14oz per day.

Five portions per day fits easily into a normal day's eating. For example:

Breakfast: Glass of fruit juice/piece of fruit alone or chopped into cereal = 1 portion.

Lunch: Piece of fruit (after sandwiches, etc.) = 1 portion.

Main meal: Two portions of vegetables (fresh, frozen or canned) in addition to fish, meat or other protein alternative and potatoes = 2 portions. Fruit-based pudding = 1 portion.

Eating that amount will not tip the scales to make you overweight because vegetables and fruit are low in calories. They are also rich in vitamins and minerals, and particularly

---

Two key ways to eat more vegetables and fruit

1 Eat a wide variety including fresh, frozen and canned, dried fruit and fruit juice (see page 69).

2 Try to eat at least five portions per day (or meet your own *Healthy Eating on a Plate* Food Goal: see page 32).

in antioxidant vitamins C, E and beta carotene (a form of vitamin A) which help protect against heart disease and cancer as part of a well-balanced diet. The fibre in vegetables and fruit could also help lower the risk of heart disease, and the mineral potassium may contribute to lowering the risk of a stroke.

Which foods are included as vegetables and fruit?

All fresh, frozen, chilled and canned vegetables and fruit with the exception of potatoes and starchy staples which we have talked about in Chapter 3 (Step One: Bread, Cereals and Potatoes). Also included are dried fruits and fruit juice, but not fruit 'drinks' and squash, which contain added sugars and other ingredients, and often not a lot of fruit juice.

Ways to eat more vegetables and fruit

BREAKFAST

• Add a portion of fruit to your breakfast cereal; eg, grate an apple or pear into your muesli, add dried fruit (prunes, apricots, raisins) to breakfast cereal and porridge.
• Serve half a grapefruit.
• Serve fresh fruit and yogurt.
• Serve dried-fruit compote.

OTHER MEALS

• Serve two portions of vegetables (in addition to potatoes) at every main meal.
• For maximum benefit eat a variety of vegetables every day.
• Make dark green, leafy vegetables and orange coloured

vegetables a regular choice for their antioxidant nutrients.
• Make orange fruits a regular choice for their antioxidant nutrients.
• Regularly add fresh fruit and/or raw vegetables to packed lunches.
• Eat more salads: seasonal vegetables and fruit, together with fish, beans, nuts and seeds, make delicious main meal salads all year round.
• Make coleslaw with natural yogurt or fromage frais instead of mayonnaise.

Healthier cooking with vegetables and fruit

Vegetables and fruit are excellent sources of vitamins and minerals. To make sure that they remain as nutritious as possible, store and prepare them using the following methods.
• Try to shop for fresh produce on a regular basis and store it properly in a cool dark place, or the fridge, as appropriate.
• Wherever appropriate, use vegetables unpeeled to retain vitamins and minerals that are just under the skin, and fibre in the skin.
• Cook for the shortest time possible.
• Cook in the minimum amount of water. Add vegetables to boiling water. Better still, steam, microwave or use a waterless cooker.
• Prepare immediately before cooking/eating.
• Don't chop fruit or vegetables into pieces that are too small because that exposes more surfaces to nutrient loss.
• Tear the leaves of green leafy vegetables rather than cutting them with a knife.
• Dress cut vegetables and fruit with lemon juice to prevent vitamin C loss by oxidation.

• Use water in which vegetables have been cooked for soups and sauces, etc because cooking doesn't destroy minerals (as it does vitamins): they just leach out into the cooking water.

• Use puréed vegetables and fruits to thicken savoury and sweet sauces instead of egg yolks, cream or a roux (flour and fat paste).

• Add grated root vegetables (carrot, parsnip, swede) to meat dishes such shepherd's pie, lasagne, moussaka and pasta sauces.

• If you make your own bread/fruit cake/fruit loaf, add grated carrot.

• Cook or stew fruit in fruit juice rather than a sugary syrup.

Raw plugs

• Try to eat some raw vegetables and fruit on a regular basis to boost your nutrient intake as cooking destroys vitamins and leads to mineral loss.

• Serve crudités (sticks of carrot, celery, cucumber, radishes and other vegetables of your choice) with tsatziki or a low-fat hummous.

• Serve a salad on the side to make a more satisfying meal of sandwiches.

• Fill pitta breads and/or tacos with crunchy raw vegetables, sprouted seeds and salad, plus a small amount of grated cheese or pulses such as chickpeas.

• If you use ready-made salads such as coleslaw, choose the lower calorie/lower-fat versions or make them go further by adding extra grated carrot, chopped celery and apple.

Budget-beating vegetables

• Choose seasonal produce because it costs less.

Fruit portions

1 apple

½ avocado pear

4 fresh apricots

1 small banana

4 tablespoons berry fruits (bilberries, blackcurrants, blueberries, gooseberries, raspberries, strawberries)

1 custard apple

4 plums/damsons

6 fresh or 4 dried dates

5 fresh or 3 dried figs

½ grapefruit

4oz/100g grapes

1 guava

2 kiwi fruit

1 orange, clementine, or other easy peeler

½ mango

6oz/175g melon

1 nectarine or peach

5 passion fruit

½ pawpaw (papaya)

1 pear

6 stewed or 4 semi-dried prunes

4oz/100g pineapple

1 pomegranate

1 sapodilla

1 sharon fruit

7oz/200g watermelon

Dried fruits: apricots, mixed dried fruit salad, dates, prunes, peaches, pears, apples. Eat them raw or stewed, in compotes, or purée and mix into yogurt.

• Take advantage of special offers, as long as the vegetables look fresh and are not damaged.
• Add lots of vegetables to stews and other meat dishes. Family members who 'don't like vegetables' might not be so reluctant to eat them if they are part of a prepared dish.
• Vegetable and lentil or bean curries are tasty, cheap and nutritious.
• Frozen vegetables can be cheaper than fresh, and there is neither preparation nor waste.

Occasional use only!

Vegetables served with rich sauces; vegetable gratins in creamy sauces with rich cheese toppings, roasted and fried (eg bubble and squeak).

Fruit served in sugar and syrupy dressings; fruit canned in syrup (choose fruit canned in natural juice); fruit desserts that usually contain a lot of sugar (eg pavlovas, gateaux, sorbets); fruit desserts that usually contain a lot of fat (eg fruit pies, fruit doughnuts etc).

Dentures, arthritis and disability

If dentures make eating raw fruit and vegetables a problem, see your dentist. It should not be a problem to eat these foods. If your dentist is unable to solve the problem, peel the fruit or vegetable and cut it into small pieces rather than go without. You could even pass them through a mouli or food processor to make purées, puddings or to serve with cereals.

If arthritis makes it difficult to prepare vegetables and fruit then don't peel them: it's beneficial to leave on the skin, where possible. Alternatively, boil potatoes in their skin and rub the skins off when they are cool enough to handle. If you

Vegetable portions

Generally, portions of vegetable are 4oz/100g, unless stated otherwise.

1 globe artichoke
5 asparagus spears
2 tbsp baked beans/lentils/chickpeas/beans/dhal etc
2 tbsp broad beans
French or runner beans
8 tbsp bean sprouts or other sprouted seeds
2 medium spears of broccoli or calabrese
cabbage
2 tbsp carrots
8 florets cauliflower
3 celery sticks
2 tbsp low-fat coleslaw
7.5cm/3in piece cucumber
fennel
leek
lettuce (all varieties)
12 poached mushrooms
½ punnet mustard and cress
onion
parsnip
3 tbsp peas (garden/processed/marrowfat)
other peas (mange tout, sugar snap)
pepper
radish
salad, large mixed or green
seaweed (nori, wakambe, kombu, Irish moss)
spinach
swede
1 corn on the cob
1 large or 6 cherry tomatoes
turnip
1 bunch watercress

are able to be a little extravagant, buy ready-prepared vegetables rather than go without.

The Disabled Living Foundation (380–384 Harrow Road, London W9 2HU, tel 0171 289 6111) offers the following advice:

1 Place cooking pans on the stove and fill with water using a jug or mug. Empty in the same way when the cooking water is cold.

2 Use slotted spoons to lift vegetables/pasta etc out of boiling water, rather than trying to lift a hot, heavy pan.

3 Cook vegetables in a vegetable or chip basket which lifts easily out of the saucepan.

4 Cook vegetables in a steamer on top of a pan of boiling water.

How to add more vegetables and fruit to your diet

BEFORE				AFTER
BREAKFAST 1 bowl cornflakes with semi-skimmed milk	fat 2g cals 160		fat 3g cals 145	BREAKFAST 1 Shredded Wheat with skimmed milk and 1 medium banana
SNACK 2 digestive biscuits	fat 5.5g cals 122		fat 0 cals 46	SNACK 1 piece fruit
LUNCH 1 individual pork pie, coleslaw, chips	fat 71g cals 1070		fat 28g cals 520	LUNCH Half an individual pork pie, 1 medium baked potato, low-fat coleslaw
DINNER Small piece garlic bread, 1 pepperoni pizza (23–25cm/9–10in) Chocolate cheesecake	fat 81g cals 1840		fat 31g cals 1470	DINNER 1 seafood pizza (23–25cm/9–10in), 1 mixed salad Summer pudding
TOTAL	fat 160 cals 3192		fat 62 cals 2181	TOTAL

BEFORE				AFTER
BREAKFAST	fat		fat	BREAKFAST
2 slices of bread with jam	9.5g		3.5g	½ grapefruit, 1
	cals		cals	wholemeal hot cross
	280		160	(or similar) bun
MAIN MEAL	fat		fat	MAIN MEAL
1 ready-made lasagne	23g		7.5g	1 reduced fat/calorie
	cals		cals	lasagne, peas, broccoli
1 chocolate mousse	545		355	1 low-fat fruit fromage
				frais
SUPPER	fat		fat	SUPPER
Cheese on toast, 2 slices	14.5g		11.5g	1 individual pot of
	cals		cals	prawn cottage cheese,
	485		270	wholemeal roll
TEA	fat		fat	TEA
1 slice chocolate fudge	34g		12g	1 wholemeal fruit cake
cake	cals		cal	
	585		290	
TOTAL	fat		fat	**TOTAL**
	81g		34.5g	
	cals		cals	
	1895		1075	

Vegetable and Fruit Recipes

Now's the time to get into the habit of including
vegetables and/or fruit at every meal or snack. There
has never been such a wide selection available, from the
humble carrot and cabbage to the exotic sapodilla.
Whichever you choose, vegetables and fruit are
excellent nutritional value for money.

**VEGETABLES
AND FRUIT**
Choose a wide variety

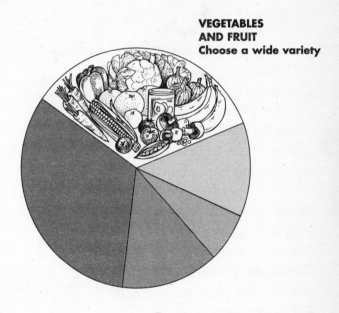

Sweet and Sour Stir-fried Vegetables with Fish or Chicken

Serves 4

Vegetables
60ml/4 tbsp sesame or vegetable oil
1 garlic clove, crushed
2.5cm-1in piece fresh root ginger, peeled and grated
1 green chilli, de-seeded and diced
1 onion, sliced
1 carrot, cut into matchsticks
100g/4oz broccoli florets
1 green pepper, de-seeded and cut into strips
150g/5oz mange tout, trimmed
1 large courgette, cut into slices and strips
6 Chinese leaves, shredded
3 large handfuls bean sprouts
450g/1lb fish (eg monk fish)/shellfish (eg prawns)/meat (eg chicken), boned and cubed

Sauce
90ml/6 tbsp soy sauce
Juice of 1 orange
2 tsp tomato purée
30ml/2 tbsp white wine vinegar
1 tbsp demerara sugar
15ml/1tbsp sherry
2 tsp cornflour mixed with 4 tbsp cold water

1 Heat all the sauce ingredients together in a saucepan over a moderate heat, stirring constantly, until the sugar has dissolved. Stir in the cornflour until thickened.

Alternatively place in a microwave-proof container and microwave on full power for 2 minutes, stirring several times.

2 Heat half the oil in a wok or other deep pan and stir fry the garlic, ginger, chilli and onion until the oil is flavoured and the onion slightly softened.

3 Add the rest of the oil and when it is hot add the vegetables (except the bean sprouts), cooking them as listed in the ingredients, in order of hardness, until cooked but not soft. Add the fish, prawns or meat for the last 4 minutes and cook through thoroughly. Add the beansprouts for the last minute of cooking.

3 Either pour the sauce over the stir fry and heat through before serving, or offer separately.

Pepper, Carrot and Coriander Soup

Serves 4

100g/4oz red lentils
1 bay leaf
225g/8oz carrots, sliced
1 red pepper, de-seeded and diced
600ml/1 pint vegetable stock
Salt and freshly ground black pepper
30ml/2 tbsp chopped fresh coriander leaves
60ml/4 tbsp natural yogurt for garnish

1 Pick over the lentils, discarding any stones. Place in a saucepan with the bay leaf and boil in twice their volume of water for about 20 minutes, until softened. Remove from the heat and remove the bay leaf.
2 Cook the carrots and pepper in the stock. Place the drained (if necessary) lentils, carrots, pepper and their cooking liquid in a food processor and blend to desired consistency, adding more stock if liked.
3 Stir in the coriander, reserving a little for a garnish, and season to taste. Re-heat. Pour into serving bowls and swirl a spoonful of yogurt into each dish, then sprinkle over the remaining coriander. Serve with plenty of crusty bread.

Broccoli Pasta with Spicy Tomato Sauce

Serves 4

Pasta
275g/10oz 1 large head broccoli, cut into florets
100g/4oz shi-itake mushrooms, sliced (discard stalks)
15ml/1 tbsp olive oil
Salt and freshly ground black pepper
450g/1lb fresh pasta shells or quills

Sauce
30ml/2 tbsp olive oil
1 onion, diced
2 garlic cloves, crushed
1 red chilli, finely diced
1tbsp chopped fresh thyme leaves
10 sun-dried tomatoes, drained and chopped
2 x 400g/14oz cans tomatoes, chopped
30ml/2 tbsp tomato purée

1 Sauté the onion, garlic, chilli, thyme leaves and sun-dried
tomatoes in the oil for about 10 minutes.
2 Add the tomatoes and tomato purée, and simmer over a
low heat for 50 minutes to 1 hour until reduced and
thickened.
3 Liquidise the sauce and reheat, ready to serve.
4 Steam or boil the broccoli in the minimum of water.
5 Fry the mushrooms in the oil and season to taste.
6 Cook the pasta in plenty of boiling water for about 6
minutes or until al dente (cooked but offering some
resistance when bitten). Drain and toss with the prepared
vegetables. Pour over the sauce and serve immediately.

Mediterranean Vegetable Pie

Serves 4

1 red onion, diced
1 garlic clove, finely chopped or crushed
5ml/1tsp fresh thyme
400g/14oz artichoke hearts in oil, drained and roughly chopped
15ml/1tbsp olive oil
150g/5oz green beans, cooked and sliced
1 red pepper, de-seeded and cut into chunks
1 green pepper, de-seeded and cut into chunks
2 courgettes, sliced
225g/8oz feta cheese
Salt and freshly ground black pepper
10 sheets of filo pastry (quarter of a 400g/14oz pack containing 40 sheets)
25g/1oz unsalted butter, melted
1 hard-boiled free-range egg, cut into 8 portions
Fresh parsley, chopped

1 Preheat the oven to 200°C/400°F/Gas mark 6.

2 Sauté the onion, garlic, thyme and artichoke hearts in the oil until the onion and garlic are soft, but not coloured.

3 Add the beans, peppers and courgettes, and cook for a further 10 minutes. Remove from the heat and stir in the feta cheese. Season with salt and pepper.

4 Brush a 20cm/8in loose-bottomed cake tin, or a baking tray and flan ring, with some of the butter. Line with eight sheets of pastry, brushing each sheet lightly with butter and arranging them so that all the base and sides are covered; allow excess to hang over the sides.

5 Place the filling in the pastry case and fold the overhanging edges across the top of the pie. Top with the remaining pastry sheets, folded lightly into an attractive pattern. Brush each layer and the top of the pie with the remaining butter.

6 Bake for 30 minutes until golden. Serve at once, garnished with the egg and parsley.

Ratatouille

Serves 4

45ml/3 tbsp olive oil
325g/12oz aubergine, cubed
325g/12oz courgettes, sliced
1 green pepper, de-seeded and cut into strips
1 red pepper, de-seeded and cut into strips
1 large onion, sliced
225g/8oz tomatoes, chopped
2 tsp dried herbes de provence (a mixture of dried herbs:
   rosemary, sage, thyme, marjoram, basil, fennel, oregano
   and mint)

1 Heat the oil in a large heavy-based pan with a well fitting
lit, add the aubergines and courgettes and fry until lightly
browned, about 10 minutes, turning frequently.
2 Add the remainder of the prepared vegetables and the
herbs, cover with the lid to enable them to continue
cooking in their own steam without the addition of further
fat. They are ready when they are just cooked, but not too
soft: about 15–20 minutes.
3 Serve on its own or as a vegetable accompaniment to
meat, fish, quiche or other main dish. Also delicious as a
filling for focaccia (small round Italian breads).

Carrot Pâté

Serves 6 (as a starter)

450g/1lb carrots
75g/3oz carrots, finely grated
3 free range eggs, separated
3 tbsp fresh chopped parsley
225g/8oz medium fat curd cheese
225g/8oz frozen chopped spinach, defrosted and drained
100g/4oz feta cheese, very finely crumbled/grated
seasoning

1 Preheat the oven to 160°C/325°F/Gas 3.
2 Boil or steam the carrots until tender. Place in a food processor with 2 egg yolks, parsley and curd cheese and purée.
3 Squeeze excess moisture out of the carrots and stir into the mixture. Season to taste.
4 Mix together the spinach, feta cheese and third egg yolk, plus some freshly grated black pepper.
5 Whisk the egg whites and fold half into the carrot mixture and the remainder into the spinach mixture.
6 Divide the carrot mixture between 6 individual no. 3 150ml/5floz ramekin dishes or a terrine. Spoon over the spinach mixture.
7 Bake in a bain marie for 35 minutes or 1hour 10 minutes (terrine) until set.
8 Remove from oven and allow to cool before *carefully* turning out. Refrigerate until ready to serve with crisp brown toast.

Fruit Jelly

Serves 4

10ml/2 tsp powdered gelatine
100ml/3½fl oz boiling water
300ml/½ pint orange juice
375g/13oz mango, peeled and sliced
2 peaches, peeled, stoned and sliced
225g/8oz strawberries, hulled and halved

1 Sprinkle the gelatine onto the boiling water and stir until dissolved. Pour the dissolved gelatine into the juice, stir well and place in the fridge to cool and set.
2 Mix the fruit together and place in a 24cm/9½in terrine or fancy mould. Pour over the cooled jelly and pack the fruit down into it.
3 Place the mould in the fridge to allow the jelly to set.
4 To serve, place a serving dish over the base of the terrine and invert so that the jelly is un-moulded; cut slices at the table.

Summer Fruits Brûlée

Serves 6

225g/8oz blackcurrants, topped and tailed
2 sprigs fresh mint
15ml/1 tbsp clear honey
120ml/4fl oz apple juice
1 tsp cornflour, mixed with 2 tbsp
  cold water
100g/4oz raspberries
225g/8oz strawberries, hulled and sliced
275g/10oz natural Greek yogurt
6 tbsp demerara sugar

To decorate
Sprigs of mint and blackcurrant leaves

1 Place the blackcurrants in a saucepan with the mint, honey and apple juice and slowly bring to simmering point. Simmer gently for five minutes; don't allow the fruit to over cook.
2 Remove from heat and stir in the arrowroot/cornflour, return to the heat and stir gently until the liquid thickens.
3 Remove from the heat and pour into six individual ramekins. Stir in the raspberries and strawberries. Allow to cool.
4 Top with the yogurt. Sprinkle over the brown sugar and place under a very hot grill until the sugar is bubbling. Return to the fridge and allow the sugar to crisp. Re-chill before serving.

Hot Fruit Salad

Serves 4

50g/2oz dried pears
50g/2oz dried peaches
50g/2oz dried apples
50g/2oz dried apricots
50g/2oz prunes
50g/2oz de-seeded raisins
1 stick cinnamon
2 cloves
2 whole green cardamoms
Juice of half a lemon
Water to cover
30ml/2tbsp brandy (for special occasions)

1 Place the ingredients in a saucepan and slowly bring to
simmering point. Cook until the fruit is plump and
softened.

Fruity Pudding Platter

Serves 4–6

4 satsumas/clementines
8 walnuts (90g/3½oz weighed in shells)
8 almonds (50g/2oz weighed in shells)
100g/4oz/4 semi-dried (ready-to-eat) figs
50g/2oz/8 semi-dried (ready-to-eat) apricots
100g/4oz/8 fresh dates
100g/4oz/12 Italian almond biscuits (*Cantuccini alla
  mandora*)

1 Put the satsumas in the centre of a flat serving platter and
arrange the dried fruit and biscuits around them.

Blackberry and Apple Summer Pudding

Serves 4

8 slices wholemeal bread from medium sandwich loaf,
crusts removed
225g/8oz eating apples, peeled, cored and cut into chunks
225g/8oz blackberries
60ml/4 tbsp water

1 Line the base and sides of a 900 ml (1½ pint) pudding
basin with 6 slices of bread.
2 Place the apples, blackberries and water in a saucepan.
Cover with a lid and cook gently for about 10 minutes
until just cooked, but not mushy. Remove from the heat.
3 Using a slotted draining spoon, transfer the fruit to the
basin. Place the remaining slices of bread on top as a lid.
4 Cover with greaseproof paper, then place a saucer on top
and weigh the saucer so the fruit juice soaks into the bread.
When cold transfer to the fridge and chill for at least two
hours, preferably overnight.
5 To serve invert the basin onto a serving plate.

Peach Medley

Serves 4

4 peaches
200ml/7fl oz white wine
25g/1oz caster sugar
225g/8oz raspberries
vanilla ice-cream or low fat iced dessert (optional)

To decorate
Borage flowers

1 Stand the peaches in boiling water for 2-3min. Transfer
to cold water then slit the skins around the circumference
and peel off the skin. Cut in half and remove the stones.
2 Put the peach halves in a saucepan with the wine and
sugar and poach for 15 min. Remove from heat.
3 Liquidise the raspberries and press through a sieve.
4 Spoon the raspberry coulis onto individual serving plates.
Top with two warm peach halves and a scoop of ice-cream.
Decorate and serve at once.

Summer Sundae

Serves 4

1 x 100g packet of ratafia biscuits
30ml/2 tbsp Fino (dry) sherry
200ml/7fl oz light crème fraîche
2 free-range egg whites
200g/7oz Greek yogurt
250g/9oz strawberries, hulled and halved or quartered
150g/5oz blueberries

To decorate
Mint leaves
1 tbsp flaked almonds, lightly toasted (optional)

1 One hour before serving, cover the base of the serving dish with the ratafia biscuits (reserving a few for decoration) and spoon over the sherry.
2 Whisk the egg whites until stiff and fold the cream and yogurt into them using a metal tablespoon.
3 Scatter a few strawberry slices onto the ratafia biscuits and pour over half the cream. Put the rest of the fruit on top (reserving a little for decoration). Pour on the rest of the cream.
4 Decorate with the reserved ratafia biscuits and fruit, mint leaves and almonds. Chill until ready to serve.

CHAPTER 5

Step Three: Milk, Cheese and Other Dairy Foods

Britain has a picture-postcard image of a pastoral land where cows graze the meadows and there is still honey, clotted cream and scones for tea. While things are not quite what they used to be in this respect, we still drink a great deal of milk and eat a large amount of dairy foods. If we are to reduce the current 40 per cent of our calories as fat to 35 per cent, or even 30 per cent, we need to cut down on our fat intake. It therefore makes sense to adjust the amount and type of milk and dairy foods we eat.

Which foods are included as milk and dairy foods?

All types of milk, including evaporated and unsweetened condensed milk, yogurt and other dairy desserts (excluding ice-cream and cream-based desserts), cheese and processed cheese and cheese spread.

> **Two key ways to cut down on dairy foods**
> **1 Eat moderate amounts** (2–3 portions per day) or meet your own *Healthy Eating on a Plate* Food Goal: see page 32.
> **2 Choose lower-fat versions whenever you can**.

Swapping to lower-fat milk

Most people use milk every day so swapping to a lower-fat and lower-calorie type of milk will make an enormous difference in the long term. Swap from full-fat whole milk (gold and silver top), if necessary, to semi-skimmed (red stripey top) or skimmed milk (blue checked top).

If you have always used whole milk, semi-skimmed does not take much adjusting to because it tastes like whole milk. Skimmed milk has a much thinner taste and takes longer to get used to. Both contain as much calcium and protein as whole milk. Calcium is particularly important in the prevention of osteoporosis (demineralisation of the bones that affects one in three women and leads to 150,000 fractures a year). Prevention starts young; studies show the more milk drunk before age 25 the lower the risk of osteoperosis. However, dairy foods remain important throughout life, as do adequate exercise, not smoking and a balanced diet. If you really cannot get used to the taste of skimmed milk for use throughout the day, you could use it in cooking and drinks where the difference in flavour will not be noticeable.

It is essential for children to have full fat milk (see Chapter 10, page 152) until they are two years old.

FAT CONTENT OF MILK

TYPE OF MILK	FAT CONTENT PER 600ML/1 PINT
Full-fat	22g/0.78oz
Semi-skimmed	9g/0.32oz
Skimmed	0.6g/0.02oz

To put this in perspective take a look at the table below which shows the grams of fat per day in a healthy diet

How much fat do you need?

	Male		Female	
	Calories per day	Grams fat	Calories per day	Grams fat
Youth 11–18	2,220–2755	86–107	1,845–2,110	71–82
Adult 19–75	2,550–2100	99–81	1,940–1810	75–70

If you want something less detailed than the above, on average an adult needs:

Male		Female	
Calories per day	Grams fat	Calories per day	Grams fat
2500	90	2000	70

Choosing the right kind of yogurt

- Choose low-fat yogurt or fromage frais (those labelled less than 1 per cent fat) in preference to whole-milk yogurt.
- Some 'creamy' yogurts are also very low in fat. Check the nutrition label for the fat content.

- Use yogurt or low-fat fromage frais instead of cream, evaporated milk or condensed milk with desserts.
- Yogurt can be used in place of mayonnaise or salad cream as a salad dressing. Flavour it with fresh chopped herbs, Tabasco, lemon juice or spices.
- Beware of luxury yogurts, some of which contain added custard and single or double cream, making them relatively high in fat.

Choosing the right kind of cheese

- Low-fat fromage frais, quark and similar low-fat soft white cheeses are the only truly low-calorie cheeses. Low-fat cheese provides 25 per cent or fewer calories from fat.
- Cottage cheese (which we usually think of as a low-fat cheese), and ricotta are medium-fat cheeses. Cottage cheese provides 35 per cent of calories from fat. Medium fat cheeses provide 25–45 per cent calories from fat.
- High-fat cheeses provide 60 per cent or more calories from fat. This includes most cheese: cheddar and other hard cheeses, blue cheeses, cream cheeses, Edam, Brie, Camembert, goats' cheeses. However, Edam and Brie are slightly lower in calories than cheddar-style.
- Try fat-reduced cheese such as half-fat cheddar.
- On the occasions when you use cheddar-type cheeses, choose mature, stronger flavoured varieties so that you can cut down on the amount used. Tasty cheeses include Farmhouse or matured cheddar, gruyère, emmenthal, Parmesan, pont l'évêque, chèvre.
- Swap low-fat and medium-fat curd cheese for cream cheese in recipes.

Choosing the right kind of cream

• Greek yogurt may contain a lot less fat (10 per cent) than double cream (48 per cent) or even single cream (21 per cent), but it still contains a lot more than low-fat yogurt (less than 1 per cent) – so don't overuse it.

• Use thick set natural yogurt instead of double cream as an accompaniment to puddings.

• Decorate desserts with piped low-fat curd cheese instead of whipped cream.

• Crème fraîche (a type of soured cream) is spoonable and contains half the fat (and calories) of double cream. Choose 'light' or reduced-fat crème fraîche which is even lower in fat and calories.

• Some artificial creams made from vegetable oil contain just as much fat as dairy cream.

Dairy Recipes

Don't let the quest for a lower fat diet put you off milk and its products. Continue to enjoy milk, cheese and so on, just adapt your recipes to include lower fat ingredients such as the following examples.

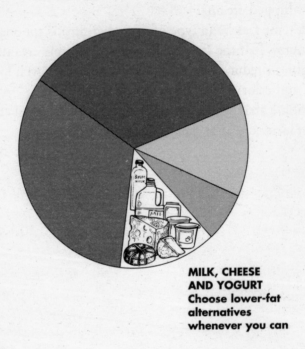

MILK, CHEESE AND YOGURT
Choose lower-fat alternatives whenever you can

Cheese and Spinach Soufflé

Serves 4

60ml/4 tbsp olive oil
40g/½oz unbleached white flour
450ml/15fl oz skimmed milk
75g/3oz gruyere cheese, grated
225g/8oz frozen spinach, defrosted and drained
freshly grated nutmeg
freshly ground black pepper
3 free range eggs, separated

1 Oil a 6½in/16.5cm souffle dish and dust with flour.
2 Stir the oil and flour in a saucepan over a moderate heat
to make a smooth paste. Gradually stir in the milk to make
a smooth sauce. Stir in the cheese and the spinach.
3 Remove from the heat and cool slightly. Beat in the egg
yolks and season to taste with nutmeg and pepper.
4 Whisk the egg whites until stiff but not dry. Fold the
whites into the soufflé mixture pour into the prepared dish.
5 Bake for 30-35 minutes until well risen and an inserted
skewer comes out clean. Serve immediately.

Mango Milk Pudding

Serves 4

600ml/1 pint skimmed milk
Pinch saffron strands
5 green cardamoms
1 ripe mango
2 free-range eggs
225g/8oz Greek yogurt
15g/½oz butter

1 Butter a 900ml/1½ pint pie dish. Put the milk, saffron
and cardamoms in a saucepan and heat to just below
boiling. Remove, cover and leave to infuse for 15 minutes.
2 Peel the mango and cube it. Put into the prepared dish.
3 Beat the eggs and stir into the yogurt. Pour the milk
through a sieve (to remove the saffron and cardamoms)
onto the yogurt, stirring to prevent lumps. Pour onto the
mangoes and set the pie dish in a roasting with hot water
two thirds of the way up the sides of the dish.
4 Bake at 180°C/350°F/Gas mark 4 for 30 minutes until
set. Either serve at once or allow to cool, then chill before
serving.

Coeur à la Creme with Raspberry Sauce

Serves 4

225g/8oz low-fat curd cheese
100g/4oz crème fraîche
2 free-range egg whites
10ml/2 tsp caster sugar
225g/8oz fresh raspberries
15ml/1tbsp cassis or grenadine

1 Line four coeur à la creme moulds (heart-shaped porcelain with holes in the base) with butter muslin and place in a dish.
2 Beat the curd cheese and crème fraîche together. Whisk the egg whites until they form stiff peaks but are not too dry. Using a metal tablespoon fold into the cheese mixture. Spoon into the prepared moulds.
3 Chill in the fridge for at least two hours before serving.
4 Puree and sieve 150g/6oz of the raspberries then stir in the cassis or grenadine.
5 Pour some sauce on individual plates. Unmould the cream hearts, remove the muslin and place a heart on top of the sauce. Decorate with the reserved fruit.

Creamy Prune Ice-cream

Serves 4-6

225g/8oz prunes
50g/2oz caster sugar
200g/7oz créme fraîche light
300ml/10fl oz half-fat extra thick cream
  or half-fat double cream
1 tsp grated orange rind

1 Soak or stew the prunes according to pack instructions.
Remove stones and purée while still warm with the sugar
and enough cooking/soaking liquid to make a thick purée.
2 Add the cream and orange rind and blend.
3 Transfer to an ice-cream maker until frozen (20-25
minutes).
Serve at once or spoon into a suitable container and freeze
until needed.

Ricotta Almond Whirls

Makes 8

25g/1oz caster sugar (optional)
75g/3oz ground almonds
250g/9oz ricotta cheese
100g/4oz dried apricot purée
1 tsp grated lemon rind
25g/1oz butter, melted
8 sheets fillo pastry

1 Pre heat oven to 200°C/400°F/Gas 6.
2 Blend the sugar, almonds, cheese, apricot purée and lemon rind to a stiff paste.
3 Brush a sheet of pastry lightly with melted butter, put a strip of filling 1in (2.5cm) from the edge nearest you, fold base over filling and fold in sides. Roll up, then curl into a coil.
4 Put on a lightly oiled baking sheet, brush lightly with butter.
5 Make the remaining whirls and bake the pastries for 12 minutes until golden brown.

CHAPTER 6

Step Four: Meat, Fish & Meat Alternatives

Meat is widely eaten and enjoyed, although not always in the right amount. A quick glance at the *Healthy Eating on a Plate Model* p.8 will show that the space on your plate for meat is smaller than most people think.

While meat may be nutritious it contains a lot of fat, especially saturated fat. As healthy eating is about controlling the amount of fat eaten, and saturated fat in particular, meat eaters have to be careful about the amount they eat.

There are plenty of alternatives to meat: poultry, fish, eggs, nuts, beans and pulses, and new foods such as Quorn and soya-based products. These alternatives will not leave you short of protein; they are all good sources of protein. Even cereals and vegetables contribute some protein and in most Western countries people eat more protein than they need.

Which foods are included as meat and alternatives?

All carcass meats (eg beef, lamb, pork, veal); meat products such as sausages, pâté, meat pastes and burgers; all types of offal; poultry; meat replacements such as soya and mycoprotein (Quorn); fish and fish products such as fish fingers, fishcakes, fish pâté, fish pastes and burgers; seafood such as prawns, scallops and oysters; eggs and egg dishes such as omelettes and scrambled eggs. Beans and pulses, canned or dried (eg baked beans, kidney beans, lentils, split peas, chick peas, pease pudding, dahl); all nuts including coconut and its products and seeds such as sesame, sunflower and pumpkin.

Does not include pies or pastries such a sausage rolls, which are composite dishes.

Simple changes for the better

- Eat lower-fat poultry instead of meat.
- Eat fish instead of meat and meat products.
- Eat dishes that combine lots of vegetables and pulses with meat. (See suggestions below.)
- Eat more alternatives such as pulses or nuts.
- Cut the fat off red meat and bacon.
- Remove the skin from poultry, as it is the fattiest part.

Two key ways to cut down on meat

1 Eat moderate amounts (2–3 portions per day) or meet your own *Healthy Eating on a Plate* Food Goal: see page 32.

2 Choose lower-fat meats whenever you can.
Eat lean meat instead of meat products. Replace at least two meat meals a week with fish, one of which should be oily fish.

- Roast meat without adding more fat.
- Choose cold meats that are cut wafer thin as this gives the appearance of greater quantity when less is used.
- Look for lean mince, labelled 'less than 10 per cent fat'.
- Choose low-fat burgers and sausages for occasional use.
- Offal is a good choice of lean meat, but it does contain more cholesterol than some other meats, so limit use. Liver is not recommended during pregnancy because it contains unacceptably high levels of vitamin A. Although vitamin A is essential for health, very high levels can be toxic to unborn babies.

Hidden fat

Meat products such as sausages, sausage rolls, pies and pâtés contain a lot of 'hidden' fat, as does most mince. Visible fat can be cut off meat such as bacon and chops, but the meat still contains additional fat.

Organic meat

Organic meat is increasingly preferable to many people because it has been produced by a system of farming that has high animal welfare standards and, like the production of organic vegetables and fruit, does not use chemicals or other practices that could harm health or the environment.

Free-range meat should also have been produced by a more humane system of farming. However, not all free-range

---

Adding fat

If you do need to add fat when cooking meat, use a small amount of vegetable oil rather than lard, dripping and other hard fats. Choose an oil high in polyunsaturates or monounsaturates such as sunflower, soya, corn, rapeseed or olive oil.

systems are as good as the name suggests.

Organic and free-range meats are more expensive, but genuine organic meat is tastier than other meat and has a better texture. If you are eating less meat in the long term the expense will be reduced.

Occasional use only!

Meat products such as sausages, pâté, meat pies and pasties, burgers, koftas, keemas, black (and white) pudding, faggots, frankfurters, haggis, luncheon meat, meat paste, polony, salami, saveloys.

Fish such as fried fish and other fish products in bread crumbs and batter.

Healthier cooking with meat

STIR FRY Small strips of lean meat can be stir fried with a wide variety of vegetables. This is a very quick method of cooking. Thin strips of lean pork and other meat can be marinated before cooking to further reduce cooking time. Using a deep-sided wok allows less fat to be used.

CASSEROLES AND STEWS Use smaller quantities of meat in casseroles replacing it with pulses (beans, lentils, chickpeas) and vegetables (carrots, swede, turnip, parsnips, potato). Make them (and stock) a day before needed, allow them to cool, then refrigerate so that the fat can be taken off the top. Re-heat thoroughly.

PASTA Ground, diced or chopped extra-lean meat can be used in pasta sauces. Include lots of vegetables (onions, tomatoes, carrots, peppers, courgettes, aubergines, leeks, cauliflower) and a small amount of meat.

FAMILY FAVOURITES   Dishes such as cottage pie, chilli con carne and lasagne can all be extended by adding beans or lentils plus vegetables.

RICE DISHES   Risotto, paella and pilau will all benefit from the addition of vegetables, pulses or nuts to complement the meat or fish.

MEAT PIES   Add beans or lentils and lots of vegetables to the meat filling. Use only one layer (topping) of pastry, rather than a base and a top, to reduce the fat content of the dish, or substitute a thick topping of mashed potato for the pastry.

ROASTING   Place the meat on a trivet in a roasting pan so that the fat drains away as the meat cooks. There is no need to add extra fat during cooking. Cover the meat with greaseproof paper and foil if it is in danger of drying out. Pour the fat away before making gravy with the meat juices.

GRAVY   Remove fat from gravy by letting it stand for a few minutes to allow the fat to rise to the top, then spoon it off. Or use a special gravy boat that leaves the fat behind.

GRILLING   Grill low-fat burgers and lower-fat sausages. Grilling is also suitable for steaks, chops and other individual cuts of meat. Remove fat after grilling and allow excess fat to drain into the grill pan to be discarded after cooking. There is no need to add fat to any of these items during grilling

Why poultry and fish are good for you

Poultry is lower in fat than meat, especially if it is organic or truly free range and has led an active life. Removing the skin will further reduce the fat content.

Fish is an excellent low-fat protein food. White fish (eg cod, haddock, plaice, whiting) is especially low in fat and rich in minerals. Oily fish (e.g. mackerel, salmon, sardines) is higher in fat, but the type of polyunsaturated fats it contains cannot be made in the body and are essential for health; hence their name 'essential fatty acids'. They may also protect against heart disease and cancer. In addition to minerals, oily fish also contains some vitamins.

Healthier cooking with poultry and fish

- To roast a chicken (or game bird) without added fat, put the breast side down in a roasting pan on a trivet. Later, invert so that the breast is uppermost for the last half to third of the cooking time. Protect the breast of game birds from drying out with a layer of greaseproof paper and foil.
- Eat fish at least twice a week in place of meat, using oily fish on at least one occasion.
- Make regular use of both white and oily fish.
- Make regular use of canned fish such as sardines, pilchards, herring which are also a good source of calcium (see page 92) because the bones are eaten.
- Choose fish canned in tomato sauce rather than oil.
- Be adventurous with fish: for example, use it to make kebabs for grilling or for cooking on a barbecue.
- Make your own fishcakes. They are both tasty and economical (use cheaper types of fish such as coley) and excellent for a snack meal or supper.
- Make fishballs (for a change from fishcakes). Combine oily and white fish in a food processor, season and mould it into balls. Dip in egg wash and roll in flour/bread crumbs (optional). Bake them on a flat baking sheet or cook them in a tomato sauce.
- Fish and chips should be only an occasional treat. If you

eat them often remove the batter from the fish as it soaks up lots of fat during cooking.

- At chip shops, ensure chips have not been cooked once and then reheated by a second frying as this increases their fat content. See also page 48.

STEAMING Most successful for both poultry and fish. Retains nutrients and flavour.

MICROWAVING No need to add fat during cooking. Especially good for poultry and fish. Cook with diced vegetables and chopped fresh herbs for extra flavour.

POACHING An excellent way to cook delicate white fish (eg plaice fillets) or whole oily fish such as salmon, trout and mackerel.

GRILLING AND BARBECUING No need to add fat to meat or oily fish. Turn frequently during cooking to prevent burning. If necessary, baste with lemon juice. Marinate meat before cooking to tenderise it and reduce cooking time. Grill fish fingers and fishcakes rather than frying them. If you do fry, use a good quality non-stick pan so that you do not have to add any fat.

STIR FRYING See under Meat, page 104.

BAKING Very good for oily fish steaks (eg salmon, tuna) or for chunky and firm white fish steaks (eg cod, halibut).

CASSEROLES AND STEWS Remove the skin from chicken or turkey before cooking. There is no need to fry the meat in fat before placing in the casserole.

> **Oily fish**
> Although oily fish such as salmon, trout, mackerel, tuna, herring are quite high in fat, they contain essential fatty acids and the fats are mainly unsaturated (unlike meat, which contains mainly saturated fat). See Chapter 7 for more information about fats.

Eggs

While eggs are nutritious and convenient, providing an alternative to meat, they are high in dietary cholesterol, and the general consensus is not to eat more than four per week, including those used in cooking.

Caution is also needed because there is still a risk of salmonella food poisoning from eggs that are not thoroughly cooked. People at particular risk are babies and children, the elderly, pregnant women and anyone who is ill. Foods containing raw eggs (eg mayonnaise, some mousses/soufflés, egg nog, some ice-cream), or lightly cooked eggs (eg soufflés, scrambled eggs, omelettes) are inadvisable for such people.

> **Nutrients in eggs**
> The main nutrients in eggs include vitamin A for healthy eyes, some B vitamins for nerves and digestion, protein for growth and repair, and iron to prevent anaemia, although the iron in eggs is not as available to the body as meat sources.

Which foods are included as nuts?

Almonds, barcelonas, betel, brazils, cashews, chestnuts, coconut, macadamias, peanuts, pecans, pine nuts, pistachio and walnuts.

Nutrients in nuts

The main nutrients in nuts include unsaturated fat (except for palm, macadamias and coconut which are high in saturated fat), B vitamins for healthy nerves and digestion, some vitamin E (in nut oils) for reproduction and healthy heart, minerals such as iron to prevent anaemia, the antioxidant minerals copper, manganese and selenium, and some fibre.

Seeds come into the nut category and these include sesame seeds, tahini (sesame seed spread), sunflower seeds and pumpkin seeds.

Nuts are nutritious but they are very high in fat and therefore very high in calories. Treat nuts with respect and use them as main meal components. Although dentists may prefer nuts to sweets because they don't cause caries (holes) in the teeth, and unlike other snacks they are high in fibre they are too high in calories for frequent snacking.

WAYS TO EAT MORE NUTS AND SEEDS
- Enjoy peanut butter sandwiches and other nut butters on bread or toast.
- Add nuts to wholemeal fruit cakes to make them fruit and nut cakes.
- Italian recipes for soups and casseroles make good use of chestnuts.
- Include more vegetarian recipes for nut burgers, loaves, rissoles, cutlets etc in your cooking.
- Decorate cakes and bakes with nuts instead of icings and frostings.
- Salted nuts can add too much sodium to the diet, so opt for unsalted.
- Try vegan 'cheeses', recipes and shop-bought items made

from nuts and from seeds.
- Use seeds (eg pumpkin and sunflower) as snacks.
- Use seeds as coating instead of breadcrumbs (eg black or white sesame seeds) where appropriate.
- Add seeds (eg poppy, caraway, linseed) to breads and spice cakes.

Beans and pulses

Pulses is the term that covers beans (see list below), peas (including chickpeas) and lentils. They are fantastically versatile in cooking, cheap and have a wonderful healthy eating profile being low in fat, high in protein and fibre. Yet most people don't eat enough of them.

Vegetarians make better use of beans and lentils, and they should eat them on an almost daily basis to avoid being over-reliant on high-fat dairy food for protein. Combined with cereals (bread and pasta) and grains (rice, etc), beans provide the building blocks of protein in the right proportions.

Canned beans are very easy to use. They may be more expensive than cooking your own but they are still a lot cheaper than meat and other animal protein foods. When cooking your own beans from dried, soak well (according to pack or recipe instructions) before cooking (except for split

---

Meeting your iron needs

The iron in meat is more easily used by the body than the iron in vegetarian foods. The same is true for zinc, another important mineral found in meat. Vegetarian sources of iron include whole grains, pulses, dried apricots and dark green vegetables. Eating or drinking foods rich in vitamin C at the same meal will help improve uptake of vegetarian iron.

> **Nutrients in beans and pulses**
> The main nutrients include protein for growth and repair, (especially important in the vegetarian diet, see below), B vitamins for healthy nerves and digestion, fibre (unlike animal sources of protein) and minerals such as iron to prevent anaemia.

red lentils) and ensure that the beans are boiled for at least ten minutes to destroy a substance that would otherwise lead to upset stomachs.

As beans and other pulses are used widely throughout the world, adding more recipes to your everyday meals is an excellent way to enjoy new and exciting dishes and sample different cuisines from around the world.

Which foods are included as beans and pulses?

Fresh, frozen, canned and dried pulses and lentils, including aduki beans, baked beans, beanburgers, gram dahl, blackeye beans, butter beans, chick peas, haricot beans, hummous, kidney beans, lentils, masur dahl, mung beans, pease pudding, pigeon peas, pinto beans, soya beans, tofu, split peas, tempeh and vegeburgers.

Ways to eat more beans and pulses

- Beans on toast is simple but nutritious.
- Try lentil curry with rice or naan bread.
- Extend meat dishes by adding beans and peas.
- Make pulses the basis of soups, stews and casseroles.
- Try out some recipes for vegetarian pâtés and terrines.
- Enjoy some classics, such as Mexican tacos and refried

beans.

- Experiment with Chinese or Japanese recipes that use tofu (beancurd) and tempeh – both made from soya beans.
- When eating out at Indian or Chinese restaurants, or ordering a take-away, try dishes based on beans, lentils or tofu.
- Choose low-fat Indian vegetarian recipes.
- If long cooking times for chickpeas or other pulses is off-putting, use more convenient canned varieties.
- Cooked lentils can be added to bread and rolls if you are a home baker.
- Use cooked beans in salads. Add celery, carrot, parsley, sweet corn, spring onions and bind with a fromage frais or yogurt dressing, or a low-fat vinaigrette.

Moves towards eating less meat

The following tables show the difference in calories and fat between eating a lot of meat and meals that contain less meat.

BEFORE			AFTER
BREAKFAST Streaky bacon bap	fat 28g cals 420	fat 5.5g cals 215	BREAKFAST 1 Weetabix with skimmed milk, 1 slice wholemeal toast, low-fat spread
LUNCH 1 sausage roll	fat 22g cals 290	fat 12g cals 320	LUNCH 1 wholemeal lean back bacon sandwich with lettuce and tomato
MAIN MEAL Steak and kidney pie, chips	fat 51g cals 900	fat 19g cals 490	MAIN MEAL Shepherd's pie, peas, cabbage
DESSERT Apple pie and ice-cream	fat 27g cals 600	fat 13g cals 420	DESSERT Fruit crumble with custard made from skimmed milk
TOTAL	fat 128g cals 2210	fat 49.5g cals 1445	**TOTAL**

BEFORE			AFTER
FRIED BREAKFAST 1 egg, 2 rashers streaky bacon, 1 sausage, 1 slice black pudding	fat 55g cals 685	fat 24g cals 365	GRILLED BREAKFAST 2 rashers lean back bacon, 1 sausage, 1 tomato, 1 poached egg
SNACK 1 tube Rolos	fat 12g cals 290	fat 6.5g cals 135	SNACK 1 crunchy bar
LUNCH 1 Scotch egg	fat 25g cals 335	fat 10g cals 280	LUNCH 1 crusty white roll with egg and salad
MAIN MEAL Quarter pounder burger in white bap, fries Thick milk shake with 2 scoops of ice-cream	fat 38g cals 755	fat 15g cals 390	MAIN MEAL Vegetarian burger, green salad, baked potato Individual low-calorie chocolate mousse
TOTAL	fat **130g** cals **2065**	fat **55.5g** cals **1170**	**TOTAL**

Meat-free days
Here are some ideas for meals that are completely meat free.

BREAKFAST Fruit juice, 1 Shredded Wheat, 1 tbsp raisins, 1 slice wholemeal toast, low-fat spread	fat 6g cals 320
LUNCH 1 bowl Minestrone soup 1 wholemeal roll	fat 6.5g cals 125
MAIN MEAL Grilled salmon steak with salsa verde, courgettes, broccoli, boiled potatoes Low fat rice pudding	fat 19g cals 560
TOTAL	fat **31.5g** cals **1005**

BREAKFAST Fruit juice, 1 scrambled egg , on wholemeal toast, low-fat spread, preserve	fat 18.5g cals 290
LUNCH Hummous with crudités (raw vegetable sticks), crispbread 1 fruit yogurt	fat 13g cals 450
MAIN MEAL Pasta with seafood sauce, salad. Hot dried-fruit compote with natural yogurt	fat 17g cals 560
TOTAL	fat **48.5g** cals **1300**

BREAKFAST Fruit juice, bowl of porridge 1 tbsp raisins, 1 slice wholemeal toast, low-fat spread, yeast extract	fat 6g cals 320
LUNCH Small wholemeal pizza topped with vegetables, salad	fat 17g cals 580
MAIN MEAL Nut croquettes/roast with carrots, broccoli and mashed potato Fruit brûlée	fat 37g cals 805
TOTAL	fat **60g** cals **1705**

BREAKFAST Fruit juice, 1 bowl crunchy muesli, poached mushrooms on Granary toast	fat 5.5g cals 375
LUNCH Baked potato, baked beans and grated cheese	fat 14g cals 380
MAIN MEAL Vegetable curry with large serving brown rice Chocolate non-dairy 'ice-cream'	fat 29g cals 1085
TOTAL	fat **48.5g** cals **1840**

Meat, Poultry, Fish, Egg and Nut Recipes

The following recipes will get you started with ways to extend meat through the use of added pulses. They may also provide ideas for ways to increase the amount of fish you eat.

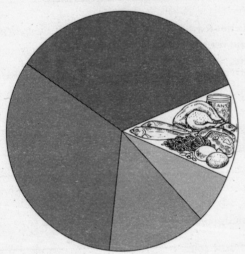

MEAT, FISH AND ALTERNATIVES Choose lower-fat alternative whenever you can

Black Bean Soup

Serves 4

1 onion, diced
1 red pepper, chopped
2 red chillies, de-seeded and diced
1 garlic clove, crushed
30ml/2 tbsp olive oil
10ml/2 tsp fresh thyme leaves
400g/14oz can tomatoes
175g/6oz black (if possible, or red) kidney beans,
   soaked for at least two hours in boiling water
   and boiled for 50 minutes
600ml/1 pint chicken or vegetable stock

1 Sauté the onion, pepper, chillies, garlic and thyme in the oil for five minutes. Add some stock and continue to cook until soft.
2 Place the tomatoes, beans and stock in the bowl of a food processor. (You may have to do this in batches.) Add the cooked onion mixture and blend to desired consistency.
3 Return to a saucepan and simmer for about 15 minutes.

Sardine Pâté

Serves 4

120g/4½oz can sardines in tomato sauce
200g/7oz low fat soft white cheese
50g/2oz fresh breadcrumbs
dash of tabasco (optional)

To garnish
Coriander or parsley leaves
Red pepper, diced

1 Clean the sardines and place in a food processor with the
remaining ingredients.
2 Blend to a smooth pâté and spoon into a serving dish.
Place in the fridge for at least one hour before serving.
Garnish and serve with melba toast and salad.

Fish Shish Kebab

Serves 4

2 medium mackerel fillets, skinned
225g/8oz coley fillet, skinned
1 tsp ground cumin
1 tsp ground coriander
15ml/1 tbsp tomato purée
¼ tsp ground turmeric

1 Place the fish, tomato purée and spices in a food
processor and blend to a smooth purée.
2 Working carefully divide the mixture equally into four
portions and form around 4 skewers.
3 Place on an oiled or buttered sheet of cooking foil under
a hot grill and cook on five minutes each side, turning
carefully.

Chilli Con Carne with Rice

Serves 4

450g/1lb lean, minced lamb
1 garlic clove, crushed
1 onion, diced
2 green chillies, de-seeded and diced
1tsp ground cumin
400g/14oz can tomatoes, chopped
400g/14oz can kidney beans

1 Sauté the lamb, garlic, onion, chillies and cumin in a
pan without added fat for about 10 minutes, stirring
occasionally. Pour off excess fat.
2 Add the tomatoes and beans and continue to cook for a
further 25 minutes. Serve with boiled brown rice.

Sausage and Bean Hotpot

Serves 4

450g/1lb pork sausages
2 onions, sliced into rings
30ml/2tbsp vegetable oil
400g/14oz can baked beans
400g/14oz can borlotti, cannellini or kidney beans
120ml/4fl oz stock
450g/1lb potatoes, sliced

1 Preheat the oven to 190°C/375°F/Gas mark 5.
2 Lightly brown the sausages and onions in the oil in the bottom of a shallow 1.5 litre/2½ pint ovenproof dish. Pour off the excess fat released by the cooking. Add the beans and stock.
3 Arrange the potatoes in concentric circles on top. Cover and bake for 20 minutes. Remove the lid and cook for another 20 minutes until the potatoes have browned.

Meatballs with Red Pepper Sauce

Serves 4

450g/1lb extra-lean minced lamb
1 large onion, chopped
2 cloves garlic, crushed
20g/¾oz fresh coriander, chopped
75g/3oz pine kernels, lightly toasted
Salt and freshly ground black pepper

Sauce
1 red pepper, de-seeded and chopped
1 onion, chopped
15ml/1 tbsp corn oil
4 ripe tomatoes, skinned and chopped
Salt and freshly ground black pepper
30ml/2 tbsp corn oil, for frying (optional)

1 Place all the meatball ingredients, except the pine
kernels, in a food processor and purée to a smooth mixture.
Stir in the pine kernels. Form into balls in the palms of
your hand and place on one side, or in the fridge, until
needed.
2 Sweat the pepper and onion in the oil until softened.
Add the tomatoes, cover and cook for about 15 minutes,
until soft. Transfer to a food processor or liquidiser and
blend to a purée. Return to the pan, season and thin to the
desired consistency with water.
3 Lightly fry, or grill, the meatballs until golden brown,
turning to cook evenly. Remove from the pan and drain on
absorbent paper. Place in a serving dish and pour over the
red pepper sauce.

Chicken in Tomato Sauce

Serves 4

4 chicken breasts, boned and skinned
30ml/2 tbsp olive oil
30ml/2 tbsp sherry
1 onion, diced
2 sticks celery, diced
1 red pepper, de-seeded and diced
1 strip orange rind, blanched
400g/14oz can tomatoes
Salt and freshly ground black pepper

1 Sauté the onion, celery and red pepper in half the sherry for about 10 minutes, until softened.
2 Add the orange rind and tomatoes. Cover and cook for a further 20 minutes. Liquidise in a food processor. Season to taste.
3 Lightly brown the chicken in the rest of the oil. When browned, add the sherry and when it is hot carefully burn off the alcohol by holding a match to the contents of the pan.
4 Pour the sauce over the chicken. Cover and cook for a further 20 minutes on a moderate to low heat.

Mediterranean Fish Stew

Serves 4

60ml/4 tbsp olive oil
1 large onion, chopped
3 garlic cloves, crushed
200ml/7fl oz tomato juice, or the juice from canned
   tomatoes
400g/14 oz can tomatoes, roughly chopped
120g/4½oz small tortellini filled with ricotta and
   spinach
700g/1½lb mixed fish, cleaned, de-scaled, filleted and
sliced (eg 1 large red snapper and 1 large grey mullet)
2 tbsp chopped fresh parsley
Freshly ground black pepper

1 Heat half the olive oil and gently fry the onion and garlic
until transparent.
2 Add the tomato juice and tomatoes, and stir in the pasta.
Cover and cook for 10 minutes.
3 Remove the lid and stir in the slices of fish. Continue to
simmer with the lid off for 15 minutes. Serve at once.

Grilled Fish Steaks with Salsa Verde

Serves 4

Fish Steaks
4 x 150g/5oz fish steaks (eg salmon, cod,
  halibut, tuna, sea bass)
Olive oil

Salsa Verde
60ml/4 tbsp extra-virgin olive oil
2 spring onions, chopped
1 garlic clove, chopped
2 shallots, chopped
2 tbsp chopped fresh coriander
2 green chillies, de-seeded and chopped
5ml/1 tsp clear honey
15ml/1tbsp balsamic vinegar

To serve
Mixed salad leaves
225g/8oz cherry tomatoes
1 large crusty loaf

1   Place half the olive oil and the remaining salsa
ingredients in a food processor and blend to a smooth
purée. Refrigerate until needed.
2   Brush the steaks with olive oil and cook on a hot griddle
for about 5 minutes on each side. Move the steaks during
cooking to achieve an attractive cross-hatch marking.
3   Place a hot fish steak on heated serving plates and top
with the salsa.
4   Place chunks of bread on the plate, drizzled with
remaining olive oil. Offer salad in separate (cold) dishes.

Fish Cakes

Serves 4

225g/8oz cooked fish, flaked (eg cod, coley, salmon)
225g/8oz cooked potato, mashed
1 tbsp chopped fresh parsley
1 free-range egg, lightly beaten
40g/1½oz white breadcrumbs
Sea salt and freshly ground black pepper
Oil for frying

1 Mix the fish and potato together. Season well, stir in the parsley and add enough egg so the mixture holds together but reserving just enough with which to brush the fish cakes.
2 When cool enough to handle, using floured hands, form into four fishcakes.
3 Brush with the egg wash and dip into the breadcrumbs.
4 Fry lightly on both sides until golden brown. Serve with peas, grilled tomatoes and potatoes.

Sliced Vegetable Omelette

Serves 4

450g/1lb small, waxy salad potatoes, cooked and
  chopped
1 garlic clove, crushed
½ Spanish onion, sliced thinly
30ml/2tbsp olive oil
100g/4oz peas, cooked
225g/8oz spinach leaves, cooked
1 medium courgette, sliced
150g/5oz sweet corn kernels
50g/2oz pine kernels
6 free-range eggs, beaten well
Sea salt and freshly ground black pepper

1 Sauté the garlic and onion in the oil in a non-stick pan
for about 5 minutes. Add the potatoes, peas, spinach, pine
kernels, courgette and sweet corn and stir to heat through.
2 Season the beaten egg and pour into the pan. Agitate the
mixture gently to allow the egg to be evenly distributed.
Leave to cook gently for 5 minutes.
3 Finish the top under a hot grill for 3 minutes.
4 Remove the pan from the heat and let it stand for 5
minutes before placing a large serving plate over the
omelette. Invert the frying pan. Cut wedges from the
omelette. Serve with mixed salad and bread.

Vegetarian Scotch Eggs

Serves 4

3 free-range hard-boiled eggs, chopped
15ml/1tbsp reduced fat/calorie mayonnaise
175g/6oz wholemeal breadcrumbs
175g/6oz ground almonds
1 onion, grated
30ml/2tbsp tomato purée
1 tbsp chopped fresh parsley
Salt and freshly ground black pepper

1 Preheat the oven to 180°C/350°F/Gas mark 4.
2 Mix the breadcrumbs, nuts, onion, tomato purée,
parsley and seasoning to make a soft paste.
3 Mix the chopped egg and mayonnaise and with floured
hands roll into 8 egg-shaped balls. Carefully form the paste
around the balls and place them on a baking sheet.
4 Bake for 20 minutes, turning once. Serve hot (with
Spicy Tomato Sauce, page 125) or cold with salad.

Nut Croquettes

Serves 4 / Makes 8

100g/4oz cashews, chopped
50g/2oz ground almonds
50g/2oz wholemeal breadcrumbs
1 onion, grated
1 tbsp chopped fresh parsley
1 free-range egg
3 tbsp sesame seeds

1   Preheat the oven to 180°C/350°F/Gas mark 4.
2   Mix the nuts, breadcrumbs, onion, parsley and egg to make a soft paste. Form into croquettes and roll in the sesame seeds.
3   Put on a baking tray and bake for 20 minutes, turning once. Serve with a salad and bread.

CHAPTER 7

Step Five: Fats

Most people eat fats on a daily basis, and most of us need to
reduce our fat intake. Because we eat fats so regularly it is
important to find ways of both cutting down the amount,
and using the right types of fat.

Which foods are included as fats?

Margarine, low-fat spread, butter and other spreading fats,
cooking oil, oily salad dressings and mayonnaise.
   A portion of fat equals:
- 1 tsp butter or margarine
- 2 tsp low-fat spread
- 1 tsp cooking oil, lard, dripping or ghee
- 1 tsp mayonnaise or oily salad dressing

Why cut down on fats?

Eating less fat is an important part of healthy eating. Fat
contains twice as many calories as starchy foods or protein.

Three key ways to cut down on fat
1 Eat minimal amounts (0–3 portions per day).
2 Choose low fat spreads and unsaturated oils.
3 Replace saturated fats with oils and fats that are
low in saturated fats and rich in monounsaturated fats
or polyunsaturated fats.

Eating less helps both weight control and health.

Eating too much fat, and saturated fat in particular, increases the risk of heart disease by raising the level of harmful blood cholesterol. Cholesterol can build up in the arteries, slowing down the blood supply to the heart or even cutting it off completely, causing a heart attack. Diets high in fat also increase the risk of some cancers.

Not all fats have the same effect. Saturated fats cause the most problems. Polyunsaturates are essential for health, and can help lower cholesterol levels. Monounsaturates seem to share the benefits of polyunsaturates. Even so, all fats should be eaten in moderation.

SATURATED FATS The type of fats we should be cutting down on are found mainly in animal foods such as meat and dairy produce. Other sources are 'hydrogenated vegetable fats and oils' found mainly in hard and some soft margarines, cooking fats, cakes, biscuits, savoury snacks, chocolate, other processed foods and some vegetable oils.

POLYUNSATURATED FATS These are the fats we need limited amounts of. They are found in vegetable oils and in oily fish, eg mackerel, herring, sardines, tuna, pilchards and salmon. Vegetable oils that are high in polyunsaturates include sunflower, soya and corn oil.

MONOUNSATURATED FATS These are found mainly in olive oil, groundnut and rapeseed oils, avocados, most nuts and some spreads.

Fats are regarded as 'extras', or additional foods to those in the four main food groups. That's because the main nutrients in fats (calories, vitamins A and D, and essential fatty acids) are adequately supplied when you make a balanced choice

from the main food groups:
1 starchy foods
2 vegetables and fruit
3 milk and dairy foods
4 meat and alternatives
– all of which are richer in vitamins and minerals. Some contain fibre, which fat lacks.

Butter or margarine?

Whichever you choose, use small amounts. Both contain the same number of calories and the same amount of fat. What differentiates them is the type of fat they contain.

Butter contains a higher proportion of saturated fat than soft spreading margarines. Hard, block and cooking margarines are mainly saturated fat. A soft spreading margarine labelled 'high in polyunsaturates' is the best choice if you want to cut down on saturated fats. You could also compare the nutrition labels of 'high in polyunsaturate' fats and choose the brand with the lowest saturated fat content. A spread that is high in polyunsaturates can also be used for baking. Alternatively, you might prefer a hard fat that is also labelled 'high in polyunsaturates'.

However, nothing compares with butter for taste and for the cooking quality it gives some dishes. But because it is so high in saturates it is best to limit its use.

For other cooking, choose a named variety of vegetable oil that is high in polyunsaturates (eg sunflower, soya) or olive

---

How many calories in your food?
Fat: 9 calories per gram
Carbohydrates (starchy foods): 3.75 calories per gram
Protein: 4 calories per gram
Alcohol: 7 calories per gram

oil which is high in monounsaturates.

If you want a spread that is lower in calories than butter or margarine, choose either a reduced-fat spread or a low-fat spread. Low-fat spreads contain only 40 per cent fat (compared with 80 per cent for butter and margarine). Consequently they contain about half the calories. Reduced-fat spreads vary in their fat content: check the nutritional label. Very low-fat spreads contain around 25 per cent fat. None of these products is suitable for cooking because of their high water content.

Cutting down on fats in the kitchen

- Limit frying, except stir frying, using the minimum amount of oil.
- Instead of sautéing, 'sweat' vegetables in a covered pan where they will cook in their own juices.
- Grill without added fat, wherever possible. Baste with lemon juice, or brush on a little olive oil.
- Don't add extra fat to roasts. The fat in the meat will roast it. If you think the meat will dry out, cover it for some of the cooking time. Start roasting poultry upside down and turn for the final half of cooking time.
- When baking, swap to lower-fat recipes such as scones (but don't then pile on the cream or butter), fatless sponges, fruit cakes; or bake yeasted goods such as teacakes, teabread and hot cross buns that are usually lower in fat.
- Cut out the use of lard and other hard fats, as far as possible. Use vegetable oils instead – even in cakes.
- Methods of cooking that don't add fat are boiling, steaming, microwaving, poaching and braising (see pages 104-108).
- Dry fry meat before adding to casseroles or other recipe dishes.

FOOD SWAP

WAYS TO CUT YOUR FAT INTAKE

	FAT SAVING, GRAMS PER PORTION	SATURATED FAT SAVING, GRAMS PER PORTION
1 egg fried for 1 egg boiled	3	1
2 slices bread with butter for 2 slices bread with low-fat spread	11	9
2 slices bread with butter for 2 slices bread with polyunsaturated margarine	0	8
Cheddar cheese sandwich with butter for cheddar cheese sandwich without butter	18	11
1 thick and creamy fruit yogurt for 1 low-fat yogurt	3	1
2 digestive biscuits for 1 banana	7	3
1 chocolate bar for 1 apple	15	9
1 packet crisps for 1 low-fat crisps	5	1
1 pork chop, lean and fat grilled, for 1 pork chop lean only	19	7
Standard beefburger in bun for low-fat beefburger in bun	5	2
100 per cent beef cheeseburger in bun for low-fat beefburger in bun	5	3
White fish in batter, fried in oil for white fish steamed or baked	33	3
Baked potato with butter for baked potato with baked beans	8	8
Baked potato with butter exchanged for baked potato with low-fat spread	15	10
1 medium portion chips fried in oil for 1 medium portion boiled potatoes	12	1
Sponge cake with butter icing for currant bun with low-fat spread	11	3
Pie with two crusts for pie with one crust	6	2
Egg mayonnaise for egg with reduced fat mayonnaise	31	4

- You may have come across these techniques in earlier chapters, but its worth repeating them here: skim fat off the top of stews and casseroles; top savoury dishes with mashed potato instead of pastry, and add more vegetables and pulses to meat-based dishes, especially red-meat dishes.

Cutting down on spreading fats

- Find some occasions when you can eat bread the Continental way – without any spread. For example, with soup, cheese or cold meat.
- Find occasions when you can eat toast without spread. For example, when topped with moist foods such as baked beans, sardines in tomato sauce or scrambled egg.
- Do not spread cheese biscuits with butter or margarine when eating them with cheese.
- Don't use spread on sandwiches; use moist, low-fat fillings instead. Or enjoy bread as an accompaniment to meals, without spread.
- Top baked potatoes with yogurt or fromage frais flavoured with herbs or spices of your choice.
- Get out of the habit of adding butter/margarine to cooked vegetables, If you must use fat, brush on a little olive oil.

You can enjoy familiar foods, but by making a few simple changes, as shown in the following tables, you can also benefit from a lower fat intake at the same time.

Fat content of ready meals
When you buy ready meals or recipe dishes choose those that contain less than 5g of fat per serving.

BEFORE				AFTER
BREAKFAST Cornflakes with whole milk, 1 slice toast, butter, marmalade, tea or coffee with whole milk	fat 14g cals 430	fat 7g cals 425	BREAKFAST Unsweetened orange juice, cornflakes with semi-skimmed milk, 1 slice toast, low-fat spread, reduced-sugar marmalade, tea or coffee with semi-skimmed milk	
LUNCH Fried sausage, fried egg and chips	fat 43g cals 700	fat 25g cals 555	LUNCH Half-fat sausage, grilled, poached egg, thick-cut straight oven chips, grilled tomatoes and mushrooms	
MAIN MEAL Large serving cottage pie	fat 22g cals 355	fat 10g cals 315	MAIN MEAL Cottage pie made with extra lean mince, added carrots, beans; served with broccoli	
DESSERT Apple crumble and custard	fat 16g cals 525	fat 8g cals 410	DESSERT Apple slices topped with no-added-sugar fruit muesli, Custard made with semi-skimmed milk	
TOTAL	fat 95g cals 2010	fat 50g cals 1705	**TOTAL**	

BEFORE			AFTER
BREAKFAST 2 wholewheat bisks, full- fat milk, 2 tsp sugar	fat 6g cals 254	fat 4g cals 160	BREAKFAST 2 wholewheat bisks, skimmed milk
2 slices wholemeal toast, butter or margarine, marmalade	fat 13g cals 297	fat 10g cals 250	2 slices wholemeal toast, low-fat spread, no- added-sugar jam
Tea/coffee with full-fat milk	fat 1g cals 17	fat 0.3g cals 11	Tea/coffee with skimmed milk
LUNCH Bacon lettuce and tomato sandwich with mayonnaise, spread with butter/margarine	fat 27g cals 450	fat 12g cals 295	LUNCH Roast chicken and salad sandwich, low-fat spread
1 x 30g packet of crisps 1 apple	fat 12g cals 195	fat 1.5g cals 155	1 low-fat fruit yogurt 1 apple
MAIN MEAL Fried cod in batter, fried chips, peas, 2 slices white bread, butter/margarine	fat 58g cals 1135	fat 20g cals 600	MAIN MEAL Cod in breadcrumbs oven baked, oven-baked chips, peas, 2 slices wholemeal bread, low-fat spread
DESSERT Blackcurrant cheesecake	fat 18.5g cals 315	fat 9g cals 240	DESSERT Low-calorie chocolate mousse
TOTAL	fat 135.5g cals 2663	fat 57g cals 1711	TOTAL

CHAPTER 8

Step Six: Fatty and Sugary Foods

We have already seen in the previous chapter that it is a good idea to eat less fat, especially saturated fat. But we also eat too much sugar. On average, 15 to 20 per cent of our calories is from sugar, whereas we should eat, at most, only 10 per cent of calories from sugar.

This might sound odd set against the popular myth that sugar is good for you – especially if you are feeling tired. Lots of people think that sugar is a good provider of energy (calories), but the reverse is true. It is a poor food, nutritionally speaking, because it provides only calories and no vitamins or minerals.

Sugar is also more likely to give you dental caries (holes in the teeth that need filling by the dentist) than:

1 naturally occurring sugars eaten as part of whole starchy foods
2 naturally occurring sugars in fruit
3 naturally occurring sugars in milk.

For these reasons it would be a good idea for most of us to halve our sugar consumption. This could also help with weight control. Sugar, confectionery, biscuit and cake manufacturers argue against the suggestion that sugary foods lead to weight problems. They say that sugar, as a form of calories, is no more likely to make you fat than any other form of calories. While technically that may be true, sugary foods (like fatty foods) are very palatable to many people, and it is easy to eat more (or too much) of a food you like. In addition, sugar does not contain any fibre to help you feel full, so you eat more calories in a smaller amount of food. For example, compare eating a popular chocolate bar with a couple of rounds of wholemeal salad sandwiches and you'll soon feel the difference.

In addition, eating sugary foods leaves less room in the diet for more nutritious foods. So cutting down on sugar (as well as fat) could improve your overall diet – and shape.

Which foods are included as fatty and sugary foods?

All the following foods are fatty and sugary. Eat only one portion per day from the list below.

Cream (and cream-based dessert toppings), chocolate and chocolate spreads, crisps, biscuits, Danish pastries, cake, ice-cream, jellies, rich sauces, fatty gravies, snack foods (such as Bombay mix and other savouries), soft drinks, sweets, sugar, sugar confectionery, sausages and fatty bacon.

You might expect the following foods also to be found in the above category, but the *National Food Guide* classifies:
• Pork pies, meat pies and pasties as composite foods, and
• Pâté and luncheon meat as meats, despite their very high fat contents.

Margarine, low-fat spread, butter, other spreading fats, cooking oils, oily salad dressings and mayonnaise are also fatty foods but they have been dealt with in the previous chapter.

Two key ways to limit intake of fatty and sugary foods
1 If you don't buy sugar, sweets, cakes and biscuits – or keep them in the home – then you can't eat them as frequently. You will be surprised to discover that if they are not there when you 'automatically' reach for them, you will have to pause, and often you will realise that you are not actually hungry. If you are, then another more suitable snack (see suggestions below) will do just as well, if not better.
2 Save up your fatty and sugary food 'treats' for the weekend (or at whatever time you would miss them most).

Sweet ways to cut down on sugary foods

- Replace sugar sprinkled onto breakfast cereal with sweetener or better still, gradually cut down on the amount you add until you no longer add any.
- Cut down the amount of sugar in tea and coffee so that you get used to drinks without sugar. If you try to cut down, but really can't do without, consider artificial sweeteners.
- Select sugar-free soft drinks and slimline mixers.
- Choose unsweetened fruit juice.
- Reduce the quantity of sugar used in cooking. Do this gradually to give yourself, and the family, time to adjust. You should eventually be able to eat most cooked fruits (except things like rhubarb) without added sugar. Alternatively, try cooking fruit in fruit juice or half juice/half water.
- Choose fruits canned in juice rather than syrup.
- Control the amount of jam, marmalade, honey, golden syrup and treacle you use. Try no-added-sugar versions of

preserves, but remember they are still sweet and calorific.

- Use dried fruit as sweeteners when cooking fruit. For example, add raisins to rhubarb or chopped dried pears to gooseberries.
- Spices such as cinnamon, mixed spice, allspice and ginger cooked with fruit help reduce the need for sugar.

Prunes as a sugar and fat replacer

Californian prune growers have come up with a way of substituting prune purée for fat when baking. Between 75 and 90 per cent of fat can be replaced with the purée. It also adds natural sweetness.

To make it, combine 225g/8oz of roughly chopped stoned cooked or ready-to-eat prunes with 90ml/6 tbsp water in a liquidiser or blender. This makes 275g/10oz of purée. Substitute on a weight for weight basis.

Hidden sugar

Sugar is an integral part of sweets, cakes, biscuits, pastries, ice-cream, desserts and many other prepared foods such as sauces, pickles, chutneys and ketchup. It also occurs in these foods and others under names such as honey, fructose (fruit sugar), concentrated fruit juice, glucose syrup and syrups.

Hidden fat

You don't have to add fat yourself for it to be present in food, especially in 'composite' foods. It is hidden away in many foods. For example, pastry is half fat and half flour, although the fat is not visible. See also Chapter 6, Step Four: Meat, Fish and Alternatives, page 104.

Cutting down on fatty foods

THE FATTY FOODS WE EAT NOW	WHAT WE SHOULD EAT
Cakes and biscuits	Less: occasional use only
Meat, fresh	Switch to lean only
Meat products: sausage rolls, pies, pâtés, pasties	Less: occasional use only
Milk	Switch to skimmed
Cheese, mainly hard	Switch to mainly low-fat
Butter	Less
Margarine	Less: switch to low-fat spreads or high in polyunsaturates margarine
Oils	Less: switch to high in monounsaturates or high in polyunsaturates
Eggs	Stay the same or no more than 4 a week

Snack Alternatives to fatty and sugary foods

When you feel a snack attack coming on, before you reach for the nearest chocolate bar, bag of sweets or crisps, consider some of these options :

- A piece of raw fruit such as a banana (see list on page 69 for inspiration).
- 2 small digestive biscuits.
- 1 fruit or natural yogurt (yogurts cultured with Bifidus bacteria – 'bio' yogurts – are naturally milder and therefore 'sweeter' than traditional yogurts)
- 1 muesli bar: search out a lower sugar version.
- 1 wholemeal currant bun.
- 1 wholemeal fruit scone, small amount of spread – no clotted cream and jam!
- 1 slice of wholemeal toast.
- 2 crispbreads or crisprolls.

- 1 oatcake.
- 2 fig rolls.
- 1 sweet biscuit.
- 1 slice malt loaf (without spread).
- Small bowl of breakfast cereal with skimmed milk.
- Small carton of fruit juice.
- Handful of raisins, dates or other dried fruit.
- 3 breadsticks (grissini).
- Serve low-fat dips with raw vegetables, crispbreads, breadsticks or lower-fat corn chips/tacos with drinks instead of nuts (especially salted) and crisps.
- Twiglets.
- Plain popcorn.
- Rice cakes and rice crackers.
- Nuts can be a good snack. Dentists prefer them to sugary foods. Unsalted nuts are best. However, remember that they are high in fat and are therefore high in calories. They are probably better regarded as an alternative to meat as a main meal component, or as a snack meal, not a nibble.

Salty snacks

At the moment we eat about 13g/½oz of sodium per day which is equivalent to 2½ teaspoons of salt. Only a fraction of that is needed and we would be better off eating far less, especially as lowering sodium intake could be of benefit in reducing high blood pressure.

Aim for no more than 6g/¼oz per day (one teaspoon) including the salt already present in prepared foods. In fact, you do not really need any added salt (unless you have special requirements) as there is enough naturally occurring sodium in the main food groups that make up the bulk of a good diet.

CHAPTER 9

Striking the Balance with Drink

Most people are interested to know how much alcohol they can drink as part of a 'healthy' diet. However, before we consider alcohol, let's look at what else you drink during the day.

Do you drink enough to meet the *Healthy Eating on a Plate* Goal of 6–8 cups/mugs/glasses of (non-alcoholic) liquid each day? (page 17)

How to drink enough liquid

- Drink plenty of water. Thirst is best quenched with water. If you don't like the taste of tap water, put it through a filter first, or buy bottled water. The latter may be expensive, but if you have paid for it you are more likely to drink it!
- Fruit juices, diluted with water, also quench thirst and are less sugary than squashes. They are better for children (see page 155).
- Skimmed milk is a good choice, if milk is liked.
- Do not drink all your 6–8 cups per day as tea and coffee because they contain caffeine (a stimulant) and they are

STRIKING THE BALANCE WITH DRINK 147

also diuretic (which causes you to lose liquids, including water-soluble vitamins).

- Find some alternatives to coffee, tea and cola (another caffeine containing drink). If you do not drink water much, find a herb or fruit tea that you like.
- Limit intake of sugary and fizzy drinks.
- Choose sugar-free drinks and mixers whenever possible.

How much alcohol can I drink?

The good news, for those who drink, is that so-called moderate drinking, which means one and a half to two drinks per day, has been associated with a longer, healthier life.

The best-known example of this is the people of the Mediterranean who drink wine as part of their traditional diet. The second point is important because a well nourished body will cope better with alcohol. So it might be necessary to add a rider and say that moderate drinking is OK, as long as it is part of a healthy diet and lifestyle (ie, not smoking and taking enough exercise). As we have seen, the healthier diet is one rich in starchy foods, vegetables and fruit, and low in fat.

Even though no disease has been associated with moderate levels of drinking, and even though moderate drinkers seem to be healthier than non-drinkers and heavy drinkers, alcohol is still a substance that the body has to detoxify, a process that needs a good supply of vitamins C, B and some minerals – hence the need for a good diet.

So, if you enjoy a drink, it would seem that you don't have to cut out alcohol, although no health experts actually recommend alcohol because of the risk of adverse effects. The exception to any possible benefit is pregnant women, (and women who think they may be pregnant or who are trying to become pregnant). No alcohol should be taken

Alcohol units
1 unit of alcohol equals =
300ml/½ pint Beer/lager
1 small glass/120ml/4fl oz Wine
1 pub measure/25ml/1fl/oz ⅙ gill Spirits
1 pub measure 25ml/1fl oz/⅙ gill Liquers (also
cocktails and other drinks)

until the fourth month of pregnancy, when one or two
drinks a week are allowed, but it is still best not to drink
alcohol at all during pregnancy.

Sensible, or so-called 'safe' levels of alcohol are up to 14
units a week for women and 21 for men. Spread alcoholic
drinks throughout the week and try to have some drink-free
days. If you are overweight, remember that alcohol contains
a lot of calories.

How to reduce your drinking

- Introduce drink-free days.
- Pace your drinking so that you drink more slowly.
- Control the amount of nibbling you do when you drink.
  Nuts, crisps and other salty and savoury snacks will make
  you more thirsty: they are designed to increase your
  drinking!
- Eating before you drink will help cut down on nibbles
  (see above) and also ensure you do not go short of
  essential vitamins and minerals.
- Alternate alcoholic drinks with non-alcoholic drinks. It
  takes your body one hour to get rid of one unit of
  alcohol.
- Make alcoholic drinks last longer by extending them
  with fizzy mineral water or mixers.

CHAPTER 10

The Right Start for Babies and Children

This book is all about the food we put on our plate. Before progressing to 'solid' food we all start life on a liquid diet. While we are not going to discuss the merits of breast feeding over the use of formula milks, or explore feeding techniques, it is worth emphasising that breast is still considered best. Whichever is used, solid foods should not be offered before four months. If the baby is not interested, try again in a few days or a week. Don't give up, but breast or formula will provide enough nourishment until the baby is six months old, when a mixed diet should be offered. Follow-on formula should *not* be used as a replacement for breast milk or formula before six months.

Four to six months

Weaning starts with semi-solid vegetable and fruit purées. Offer a little on a spoon and do not mix with milk or other drinks in a bottle. Do not add sugar or salt; babies accept bland foods. This applies up to the age of two and beyond, if possible.

Purées should be of a sloppy consistency. Cook the foods

in a minimum of water (or steam) until the fruit or vegetables are soft, then press through a sieve or use an electric blender. Add some of the cooking water (or previously boiled water or milk) to make the purée. Fruit and vegetable purées can be made in batches and frozen in ice-cube trays. Once frozen, remove and store in freezer bags or boxes.

When preparing foods for babies be scrupulously hygienic.

First solids

- Cooked apple and pear purées, finely mashed/sieved banana, finely mashed/sieved avocado.
- Cooked purées of carrot, potato, sweet potato, peas, spinach or squash.
- Baby rice or home-cooked puréed rice/cornmeal/ sago/ millet (ie non-wheat cereal), mixed to sloppy consistency with breast milk, formula or boiled cooled water.

The baby will still continue to have breast or formula feeds and cooled, boiled water can be offered as a drink, if necessary.

Six to nine months

At this age you can start to use food mashed with a fork or minced rather than sieved, puréed foods.

Introduce the following foods. If they are not liked, offer them again in a couple of weeks' time. Continue with hygienic practices and cooking in the minimum of water.

Suitable foods

- Mix fruits and vegetables (as soon as they are accepted without problems).
- Mixed fruit purées: apple/pear, apple/pawpaw(papaya), apple/peach/nectarine, apple/guava, apple/mango. Cook the

Vegetarian babies

Protein sources should be mixed to ensure the body gets all the building blocks of protein that it needs in the correct proportions: that is, cereals and pulses, or cereals and nuts, or pulses and nuts. Never give babies, toddlers and small children whole nuts because of the risk of choking. Vitamin C-rich foods (ie vegetables and fruit or juice) should be offered at each meal to ensure iron uptake from vegetable foods.

fruits together for a mixed fruit purée.

• Introduce purées of soft cooked dried fruits, and 'dilute' them with yogurt.

• Mixed vegetable purées: combining already frozen single varieties of vegetable cubes may be easier than cooking and puréeing together. Introduce new varieties such as cauliflower, courgette, green beans, celeriac, sweet corn.

• Yoghurt (unsweetened) plain and mixed with fruit purées, fromage frais.

• Purees of lean meat (including liver), poultry, fish and split peas or lentils, may now be offered.

• From around seven months, bread and breakfast cereals based on other grains (wheat, oats) can be introduced. Special baby mueslis are available; choose versions with no added sugar.

The baby will still continue to have breast or formula feeds. If breast milk is the baby's main drink, supplements of vitamins A and D should be given from six months up to two years of age, or five years, if necessary.

Drinks can be offered from a cup from six months. Cows' milk can be introduced for cooking and possibly on breakfast cereal from six months.

Milk: full-fat or lower fat?

Babies and toddlers need full-fat milk until they are two years old because for many, milk is one of their main foods and they rely on it for most of their calories. Between the ages of two and five years, if they are eating a varied diet, semi-skimmed milk can be introduced. Skimmed milk can be introduced from the age of five.

Cooled, boiled water should be offered as a drink. If fruit juice is used make sure it is well diluted with cooled, boiled water, and use three to four parts water to juice. Serve fruit juice only with meals to reduce the risk of tooth decay, and do not give it in a bottle or at bedtime.

Nine months to one year

Now you can introduce slightly lumpier (ie chopped) foods: the aim being to have the baby weaned on to foods that the rest of the family eat (with the exception of junk foods and overly spiced foods, etc) from the age of one.

Increase the range of foods offered to include eggs and fish, but do not introduce shellfish until the age of two.

Try other fruits such as citrus fruits, berries and mango.

Finger foods can be introduced now, such as fingers of toast, bread, carrot, apple, pear and banana. Supervision is essential because babies easily choke on these foods.

The baby will still continue to have breast or formula feeds: about 600ml/1 pint a day or more, if required. The aim is to introduce cows' milk gradually so that by the time the baby is one year old, ordinary milk can replace breast or formula milk. About 600ml/1 pint of cows' milk per day is recommended in addition to normal mixed feeding. However, breast feeding can continue if preferred.

Cooled, boiled water can be offered as a drink, if necessary. If fruit juice is used, see above. From one year, drinks should be taken from a cup, not a bottle.

One year old

By this age the baby is now called a toddler (even if not walking!), and s/he should be enjoying three meals a day, plus up to 600ml/1 pint of milk. If babies are hungry, or if they do not seem able to eat much at meal times (and babies' stomachs are small and their calorie needs great), between-meal snacks can be given. However, make these as nutritious as possible, not crisps and chocolate which do not provide enough vitamins and minerals to cover the needs of a rapidly growing baby.

Babies need far more nutritious foods than adults, so it is important to make sure that all three meals and snacks are packed full of nutrients. If you find snacks result in lack of interest in food at meal times – especially with babies that usually eat a hearty meal when hungry – then do without. Often babies will just want to eat because they see you eating something and they want to join in. Sometimes just a taste or two, if appropriate, will suffice.

Up to 600ml/1 pint of cows' milk per day is recommended in addition to normal mixed feeding. Cooled, boiled water can be offered as a drink, if necessary. If fruit juice is used make sure it is well diluted with cooled, boiled water.

Handy snacks
• Wholemeal sandwiches, or fingers of bread spread with peanut butter, a little spread and yeast extract or soft cheese.
• Bananas.
• Vegetable sticks.
• Raisins.
• Wholemeal fruit buns.

More tips for 1 year onwards
- If vegetables are rejected, try them grated, eg carrots or chopped tomatoes, or hide them in stews and soups.
- Do not add sugar to drinks. Limit soft drinks to meal times; water or milk between meals.
- Discourage frequent snacks on fatty or sugary food.
- Discourage feeding from a bottle after one year.
- Do not add fat when cooking food for babies and toddlers.

Commercial foods

Commercial baby foods are available from weaning through to toddler food. These are convenient and have been prepared in hygienic conditions. However, if you want your baby/toddler to become used to home cooking then, if you can find the time, try to prepare as much of the food as possible yourself. It is certainly cheaper.

Toddlers

Toddlers describes children aged from one to three years.

Worrying about whether children are eating enough of the right sort of food is of universal concern to parents. With toddlers, the anxiety is magnified three times a day as the food flies in all directions while an 18-month-old learns to use a spoon. Combined with the natural stubbornness of most toddlers, which means that many of them refuse to eat at meal times, most parents are convinced, at one time or another, that their child has eaten next to nothing. If your child is full of energy and healthy s/he is probably eating enough.

Toddlers also 'go off' their food when teething and they may just not feel hungry. Try offering another meal again (do not reheat food) in an hour or so. If they are still not hungry, leave it until the next usual mealtime. They won't starve themselves, even though it is worrying and annoying when you have prepared the food and have to throw it away.

While toddlers should be eating the same food as the rest of the family, this does not apply to fats, before the age of two years. Long-term studies are needed to find out exactly what is the best type and amount of fats for babies and children. Meanwhile, they should have full-fat milk and dairy foods until they are two years old. Between two and five years there can be a gradual switch to the proportions of food found on the adult plate.

That said, do not force a child to eat something it obviously dislikes; respect children's food preferences.

Ways to serve up good foods for toddlers
MILK Needed for calories and calcium for healthy bones and teeth. Other sources of calcium include yogurt, fromage frais, cheese, canned sardines and green leafy vegetables. Serve with breakfast cereal, as a milk shake, cooked in puddings, mixed into mashed potatoes and other vegetables.

Drinks for children
Fruit juices should be diluted with water for babies and young children. Neither juices or sugary drinks should be left in bottles or other feeders because this can cause tooth decay. Fruit juice is best taken with meals and not sipped in between because this limits the number of times sugary substances enter the mouth. The risk of tooth decay increases with the frequency of sugary drinks and foods entering the mouth.

BABIES	NUMBER OF PORTIONS	
	Milk and dairy foods	**Bread, potatoes, pasta and other cereals**
4–6 MONTHS	**600ml/1 pint breast or formula per day.**	Mix smooth non-wheat cereal eg baby rice with milk. Purée starchy vegetables.
6–9 MONTHS	**Around 600ml/1 pint breast milk, formula or follow-on formula per day. Hard cheese may be cubed, grated or used as finger foods.**	2-3 portions per day. Introduce wholemeal bread and wheat cereal. Start to give lumpier foods and finger foods, eg toast.
9–12 MONTHS	**600ml/1 pint breast or follow-on formula per day. Use breast, follow on or cows' milk to mix cereals and solids**	3–4 portions per day. Encourage wholemeal products; avoid foods with added sugar. Starchy foods can be normal adult texture.
1 YEAR	**Minimum 350ml/12 fl oz milk per day or 2 portions dairy produce.** Whole milk may be used as a drink. Introduce soft cheeses after 1 year. Lower fat milk only for cooking.	**Minimum 4 portions per day.** At least one serving at each meal. Discourage high-fat foods (crisps, savoury snacks and pastry).

NUMBER OF PORTIONS

Vegetables and fruit	Meat and alternatives	Other information
Soft cooked vegetables and fruit, smoothly puréed.	Soft cooked lean meat or pulses, sieved.	Low sugar desserts, eg fromage frais with fruit for occasional use.
2 portions per day. Raw soft fruit and vegetables, as finger foods. Cooked vegetables and fruit can be mashed for coarser texture.	**1 portion per day.** Soft cooked puréed or minced meat, fish, pulses. Chopped hard-cooked egg may be used as finger food.	Restrict fruit juices to meal times only. At other times offer milk or water. Encourage savoury rather than sweet foods.
3–4 portions per day. Lightly cooked or raw foods. Chopped or finger food texture suitable. Unsweetened orange juice with meal.	**Minimum 1 portion per day, or two from vegetable sources.** Use lean meat. For vegetarians use mixture of vegetable and starch foods.	Small amounts of butter or margarine. Small amounts of jam on bread, if baby will not eat bread on its own. Limit salty foods.
Minimum 4 portions per day. Try unsweetened fruit if vegetables are rejected. Food can be adult texture.	**Minimum 1 portion per day, or 2 from vegetable sources.** Encourage low-fat meat and oily fish eg sardine, herring, mackerel.	Encourage three meals per day. No more than 600ml/1 pint milk as it will stop appetite for food. Bread or fruit if hungry between meals.

BREAD AND CEREALS For breakfast cereal and bread, choose the wholemeal versions without added sugar and salt (although bread always has salt added). Wholemeal cereals (including pasta) are rich in vitamins and minerals and fibre, and are also good energy foods. Cereals also include (brown) rice.

Serve bread as finger food, as mini sandwiches, crumbled into toppings for vegetables and baked pasta dishes. Serve plain boiled rice and pasta with stews, casseroles and meat or vegetarian sauces.

POTATOES Very versatile and rich in vitamins and minerals, especially if unpeeled as the nutrients are just below the skin. British people eat so much potato they derive a lot of vitamin C from them, even though they are not a particularly rich source. Sweet potatoes are especially good because they contain beta carotene (see broccoli, below). If potatoes are not your particular staple food, then serve pasta or rice (see above) on a daily basis.

Serve boiled, steamed or mashed, as a vegetable in their own right. Use as toppings for vegetable dishes and meat or fish pies. Use to thicken soups and casseroles. Serve baked potatoes with baked beans, grated cheese or vegetable sauces.

BROCCOLI Contains beta carotene, a protective antioxidant vitamin. All green leafy vegetables, orange (red and yellow) vegetables and fruit contain beta carotene which is also a pigment responsible for their natural colour. Broccoli, and other cabbages, also contains other substances that may be involved in producing enzymes to prevent or fight cancer.

Serve mashed with potato to dilute the taste, liquidised in stews or soups, chopped into tiny pieces in pasta sauces, macaroni cheese, and in stir-fries which make good finger foods (when cooled). Serve in a cheese sauce (as a change from cauliflower cheese).

CARROTS Rich in vitamin C, fibre and beta carotene (see broccoli, above).
Serve raw in vegetable salads, as a finger food to snack on, and as for broccoli.

BANANAS An ideal sweet portable snack. Being a starchy fruit they are filling. They are also rich in vitamins.
Serve just unzipped, or mashed and mixed with yogurt, fromage frais or custard; sliced onto breakfast cereal and into fruit salads or grilled and baked for pudding.

ORANGES Like other citrus fruits, one of the best sources of vitamin C, essential for protection against colds and other illnesses. Oranges also contain beta carotene (see broccoli) and help absorb iron from vegetarian foods.
Serve cut into segments and eaten as a pudding (easy peelers are good for this), put into fruit salads and bake into puddings.

FISH An excellent source of protein. White fish is easily digested; oily fish contains essential fats (because they cannot be made in the body) which are needed for growth and health. One advantage of fish over meat is that the fats it contains are not saturated. (Saturated fats are linked to heart disease in later life.) However, fish is not rich in iron and zinc; meat is a good source of these minerals. So, for a balanced diet, include both fish and lean meat. Liver is especially rich in minerals.
Serve meat and fish in their own right, or cooked in pasta sauces, casseroles, fish pies, fishcakes, fish fingers.

SPLIT PEAS These and other pulses, such as lentils and beans, provide protein from a vegetarian source, and also iron and fibre. Iron from vegetable sources is better used by the body if taken with orange juice or oranges.
Serve in dahl-type mixtures (soupy sauces), or put into cottage pies, or purée and use as dips with carrot sticks.

PEANUT BUTTER Peanut butter and other finely ground nuts can be used after six months of age, but never give toddlers and small children whole nuts because of the risk of choking. Combined with grains (bread) peanut butter is a good source of protein, fibre and fats.
Serve sandwich style, stir into sauces for pasta or chicken, mix into home-made puddings, cakes and muesli bars.

DRINKS Remember to offer sufficient drinks throughout the day (in addition to milk). Water is best for quenching the thirst.

Allergies

Beware of cows' milk, bread, oranges and nuts: these foods are the most common causes of allergic problems, such as eczema, in infants. Keep an eye on your baby when you first introduce these foods. Seek specialist advice from your GP and/or health visitor if you suspect allergic reactions in babies and toddlers.

Eggs and children
If you are wondering why eggs are not listed as a good food, the government health warning associated with the risk of salmonella for vulnerable groups such as the very young is still in force. If you use eggs, the yolks and whites should be cooked until solid.

Encouraging children to eat vegetables

As pre-school and school children become more aware of, and possibly influenced by, the pressure of advertising aimed at them by producers of confectionery and junk food, so they will start to reject vegetables and other plain, nutritious foods. Peer pressure may also influence them into thinking that vegetables are 'yuck'. Here are some suggestions to help maintain their vegetable intake.

• Add grated carrot, chopped celery, shredded cabbage, broccoli florets or other vegetables to mince when making burgers or shepherd's pie.

• Add brightly coloured vegetables such as peppers, tomatoes and sweet corn kernels to ready-made/bought pizzas.

• Add diced carrot, peppers, chopped tomatoes and peas to spaghetti bolognese sauce.

• Add sliced and grated vegetables to sandwich fillings, mixing them with items such as egg, grated cheese and peanut butter.

• Serve meat and vegetable kebabs from the barbecue instead of/as well as burgers and sausages. Or thread cut-up burgers and sausages onto kebabs with vegetables.

• Add other vegetables to mashed potato, eg swede, carrots, parsnip, celeriac, turnips.

From seven years

Children will now begin helping themselves from the fridge or cupboards (if allowed) and may be spending pocket money on chocolate, sweets or other sugary and fatty foods. Try to keep sweets to meal times only and make sure they brush their teeth after eating sweets. Explain why these foods are for occasional use only and encourage other treats instead of these foods, such as comics, badges, stationery, hair slides and other small items. If children become fussy about vegetables, see above.

Packed lunches may help influence their food intake for the better. Include a wholemeal sandwich or roll spread thinly and filled with lean meat, tuna, sardines, Marmite and salad, cheese extended with grated carrot. Add a piece of fruit and a fromage frais or yogurt and a wholemeal currant bun, plus a carton of unsweetened juice, or milk.

From 11 years

Children are growing fast at this age and need lots of calories. Ensuring that they eat lots of starchy foods such as bread, pasta, potatoes and rice, plus vegetables and fruit, will fill them up in the most nutritious way. As bones are growing fast, try to include some dairy food. Iron is especially important when girls start to menstruate.

As many young people become vegetarian at this age, include other sources of iron in their diet such as eggs, pulses, green leafy vegetables and fortified breakfast cereals. Encourage orange juice with these meals, or citrus fruits, to help the body absorb the iron.

Explain to them that sandwiches, dried fruit, fresh fruit, milk shakes, low-fat wholemeal biscuits, cakes and buns are better than confectionery, chocolate, and so on. Even encourage the myth that chocolate gives them spots!

Adolescents

Once children become teenagers it is far more difficult to influence what and when they eat. They will be taking more meals outside the home and girls, in particular, may be dieting. It is a difficult time, because their needs for nutrients are still high as growth is continuing, if not quite as rapidly as during infancy. General well-being and vitality will be lowered if they do not eat well.

Probably the best ways to encourage continued good eating habits is to:

1 Appeal to their vanity, explaining that their appearance and body shape will be far more attractive if they eat the right foods. Explain that dieting does not work; it ultimately leads to more weight gain. Exercise is a better way of influencing body shape and composition.

2 Appeal to their conscience, concern for the environment or feelings about animal welfare. Suggest that starchy foods and vegetables and cereals, vegetarian alternatives to meat such as pulses, generally speaking, do not cause environmental problems and are a fair way of sharing the world's food resources.

The ten worst foods for teenagers (and all ages!)

1 Sugar Whether added to drinks or on sugar-coated breakfast cereals, or as an ingredient in processed foods.

2 Salt Don't add it during cooking or use a lot of processed foods that are high in salt. (Babies and toddlers don't need added salt.)

3 Fizzy drinks Most (except water) are too high in sugar, lack vitamins and minerals and encourage tooth decay. The longer the milk teeth last the better as this 'saves' second teeth and ensures they are positioned well in the mouth. If you give fizzy drinks now it will be impossible to ban them once the second teeth arrive.

4 Biscuits Stick to plain digestive types. Or let them eat cake: home-made wholemeal fruit cake is very nutritious; low-fat scones and buns are acceptable.

5 Puddings Eaten at every meal is a bad habit. Instead give fruit or yogurt or a low-fat iced dessert.

6 Sweets and chocolate have no nutritional value.

7 Pastries, pies, chips, patties, samosas, spring rolls are all too high in fat.

8 Ready meals or recipe dishes Choose carefully as most are very high in fat. If used, should have lots of vegetables or potatoes added.

9 Burgers and take-aways Tend to be very high in fat. Many are fried and eaten with other fatty food, such as chips.

10 Fried foods Keep to an absolute minimum. The only type of fat that is essential to health is found in oily fish, green leafy vegetables and vegetable oil.

Recipes for Babies and Children

All the following dishes are suitable for children from the age of six months, if your baby is well advanced with solids and mixed feeding. Prepare to the consistency that suits the baby: that is, either sieve, mouli, purée – or just chop/dice for age one year onwards.

The number of portions yielded will vary according to the child's appetite. Freeze extra portions for later use.

Poached Fish

225g/8oz salmon fillet (skinned and boned),
  or other fish of choice
400g/14oz potatoes, peeled
350g/12oz can sweet corn in water (no added salt
  or sugar)
100g/4oz peas (shelled weight)
225g/8oz courgettes, unpeeled and sliced
1 tbsp very finely chopped fresh parsley

1 Steam the salmon for six minutes and flake into a bowl.
2 Boil the potatoes and mash (but not too finely).
3 Put the sweet corn in a blender and purée, then pass through a mouli (or sieve, which is harder work) to remove the husks.
4 Steam the peas and the courgettes for five minutes. Mash.
5 Mix all the ingredients together. Make a final check for fish bones before serving. Freeze the remaining portions.

Lamb Casserole

150g/5oz neck fillet of lamb, chopped
2 carrots, grated
3 medium potatoes or sweet potatoes,
   scrubbed and sliced
1 courgette, sliced
1 leek, washed, trimmed and sliced

1 Place the potatoes in the base of a heavy based saucepan.
Lay the lamb and slices of leek and courgette on top. Add
the grated carrot.
2 Cover with water and bring to simmering point. Cook
gently, topping up with water if necessary, for 35 minutes.
3 Cool quickly and portion for freezing.

Chicken and Rice

50g/2oz brown rice
1 free-range chicken breast, skinned and boned
1 courgette, unpeeled and sliced
100g/4oz swede, peeled and chopped
1 carrot, grated
50g/2oz peas

1 Wash the rice and cover with 5cm/2in boiling water in a
saucepan. Cook for 12 minutes.
2 Slice the chicken and add to the rice, together with the
remaining ingredients. Cover the pan and simmer for 20
minutes.
3 Remove from heat. Cool quickly and divide into
portions for freezing.

CHAPTER 11

The Winning Formula: Changing What You Eat

Most people need a good reason to change what they eat. Perhaps your doctor has said that you should lose weight for health reasons. Perhaps you have a family history of heart disease, strokes and some cancers. Perhaps you have high blood pressure or a higher than desirable blood cholesterol level. Perhaps you suffer from indigestion and heartburn, or constipation, because of the food you currently eat. Or maybe you are just sedentary and therefore at risk of becoming overweight.

Whatever the reason, a change for the better in diet will benefit your health and well-being in several ways.

While you might want to make the change yourself it is very difficult to do it alone. Once you have decided that you want to change then you will need the support of a partner, family or friends, and maybe even some professional help from your doctor, or a dietitian.

Talk about what you have decided to do with the person or people you take most of your meals with. This may be someone other than a partner. It could be a friend, parents or work colleagues. If possible, get someone to change with you. It's easier if everyone is eating the same food.

Learn to be (politely) assertive when others try to persuade you to give up what you are doing, or to eat extra portions or food you do not really want, or to share their over-indulgences. You are not a killjoy if you say 'No thanks'. You can still join in the fun, but you don't have to do – or eat and drink – exactly what they do.

Before you start

To find out what changes you need to make see, Chapter 2, page 32 and reaffirm your goals here.

Your *Healthy Eating on a Plate* Food Goal
Fill in the tables below

What I eat now Number of portions:					
Bread	Fruit	Milk	Meat	Fats	Fatty/sugary

Healthy Eating on a Plate Food Goal Number of portions:					
Bread	Fruit	Milk	Meat	Fats	Fatty/sugary

Familiarise yourself again with the foods that make up the main food groups. Think through the targets in each of the four main food groups, in your personal table above, and decide how you can best make the changes. For example, if you need to eat more vegetables and fruit, would you prefer to increase the number of occasions on which you eat them during the day? Or is it more convenient for your lifestyle to eat larger portions?

Look at the extras. It is likely that most people will need to eat fewer of these foods. Regarding them as 'treats' from now on may help. Work out what you will replace them with on a daily basis. Look at the healthier snack options on page 144. Plan ahead for times when you will be tempted to eat them out of habit, and plan ahead (see below) to have an alternative to hand. Eat treats on the occasion(s) you would most miss them.

Many people may also need to reduce their intake of alcoholic drinks. Re-read the section on ways of coping with this, on page 148.

What we eat today, compared with what we should eat

The table on page 170 is taken from the government's National Food Survey, which shows the average diet of the British population eaten at home. It shows the amounts and type of food eaten at present, as a national average, and the changes that would result if adjustments were made to meet recommendations for a healthier diet. It is far from ideal and you would be better advised to follow the six steps to a healthier diet outlined in this book. However, it is interesting to look at how just a few minor adjustments can tip the balance in favour of a healthy diet.

WHAT IS EATEN NOW	WHAT MIGHT BE EATEN
1 glass whole milk a day	½ glass whole milk a day
1 glass semi-skimmed milk a day	1¾ glasses semi-skimmed milk a day
1 tbsp cream a day	½ tbsp cream a day
Enough cheese to fill 2–3 sandwiches a week	Enough cheese to fill 1–2 sandwiches a week
2 portions of beef and lamb a week	2 portions of lean meat a week
3 portions of pork and poultry a week	3 portions of lean pork and poultry a week
7 portions of other meat and meat products a week	3½ portions of other meat and meat products a week
1 portion of white fish or fish products plus 1 or 2 portions of oily fish a week	1 portion of white fish or fish products plus 1 portion of oily fish a week
1 egg a week	1 egg a week
Enough butter or margarine to spread 3 slices of bread a day	Enough butter/margarine to spread 1½ slices of bread a day
Enough low-fat and reduced-fat spread to spread 1 slice of bread a day	Enough low-fat and reduced-fat spread to spread 2½ slices of bread a day
4½ tbsp of vegetable oil and 1½ tbsp of other fats a week	9 tbsp of vegetable oil and ¾ tbsp of other fats a week
1 portion (2 egg sized) potatoes a day	3 egg sized potatoes or 1 medium a day
1 medium portion of chips or 2 potato croquettes a week	1 small portion of chips or 1 potato croquette a week
2–3 portions of vegetables a day	4 portions of vegetables a day
1½ pieces of fruit a day	2 pieces of fruit a day
3 slices of bread (of which 1½ wholemeal) a day	4½ slices of bread (1 wholemeal) a day
3–4 biscuits a day	1–2 biscuits a day
6 tsp sugar or thick spread of preserves for 2 slices of bread a day	5 tsp sugar or thin spread of preserves for 2 slices of bread a day
2 cans soft drink a week	1 can soft drink a week, plus any amount of sugar-free drinks
1 small bar chocolate a week	¾ small bar chocolate a week
1 bowl breakfast cereal a day and 1 serving pasta or rice a day	1 bowl breakfast cereal a day and 1 serving pasta or rice a day

Diversionary tactics

If there are particular times in the day or particular events at which you will find it especially difficult to change your eating or drinking habits, think ahead about how to avoid those situations. For example, if evenings at home in front of the TV are difficult to get through without nibbling on extras, take up knitting so that you are busy and your hands are occupied.

More seriously, ask yourself if you are really hungry when you munch on biscuits or savoury snacks between meals, or whether you are just eating out of boredom or because you like the comforting feeling of eating. Health professionals refer to this as 'mouth hunger' as opposed to 'stomach hunger'. You need to recognise the difference yourself and find ways of combating mouth hunger. Chew gum, for example, instead of eating.

Similarly, some people find it difficult to see a cake shop or sweet shop without going in and buying something. If this is the case, avoid the shop, or buy something really plain, such as a plain currant bun or a wholemeal bread roll.

Consider an evening class instead of spending your evenings munching in front of the TV. If you can't get food off your mind, take up a cookery class, preferably one that deals with healthier cooking methods, and learn to cook tasty and healthy food for yourself. Or you could tackle the DIY jobs that you have been putting off. Take up an exercise class or sport. Telephone a friend or relative for a chat; or find someone who agrees to support you.

While the aim is to adopt healthier eating habits for the long term, don't view this as a lifetime of deprivation. Of course there will be times such as Christmas, birthdays and other social occasions when you will – along with everyone else – abandon your generally good eating habits. Don't worry about it; enjoy it. It is the long term that counts.

However, if you unintentionally lapse on a regular basis, you might need to find ways of reminding yourself of the positive reasons for change. Alternatively, you might need some inspiration with new recipes or foods that fit your healthy eating plan. Think about all the foods you enjoy rather than the extras you are missing.

If you need a reward for the changes you have made then give yourself one. For example, save the money you would have spent on 'extras' to accumulate enough for new clothes, shoes or towards a holiday.

Planning Ahead

Work out a shopping list to avoid impulse buying and help you stick to your resolution to change what you eat. You might find it easier to have a weekly shopping list for groceries and a more frequent, perhaps twice weekly, list for perishable foods such as milk, vegetables, fruit and bread (although you can keep some of these in the freezer).

Writing a shopping list will also help you plan meals in advance. This has several advantages. It helps you stick to what you plan to eat. In the long run it should save you money because you only buy what you need. However, do remain a little flexible to take advantage of bargains. For example, if you planned to buy and cook cauliflower, swap it for cabbage or broccoli if it seems fresher or is a better price. Alternatively, there might be a special offer on a store cupboard item such as canned pulses or pasta that you could buy for later use.

Planning ahead will also help you cut down on waste and make most economical use of foods in other ways. For example, if you have a joint of lamb on one day, the following day you could cook a shepherd's pie and on the third day you could have cold meat and salad such as home-made coleslaw and baked potatoes.

Eat before you go shopping: that way you will not succumb to the confectionery at the checkout.

Decide for yourself

Only you can decide that you are going to change your eating habits for the better. Find a really good reason to do it, and then try to get everyone on your side to help you – or better still join in with you.

Reasons for change

- You want to look and feel better.
- You want to give your children a better start in life (with healthy eating habits).
- You want to find a way of eating that will help you become slim and/or stay slim.
- You want to minimise the chances of having a heart attack or cancer or other disabling condition when you are older.
- You are expecting a baby, or planning to become pregnant, and you want to give your baby the best start.
- You want to boost your immunity by eating food rich in vitamins and minerals so that you don't catch lots of colds in the winter.
- You don't want to make junk food manufacturers any richer.
- You object to the way confectionery and junk food manufacturers spend your money advertising nutritionally poor quality food on children's TV – so you are not going to spend any more with them.
- You don't ever want to diet again. Instead, you want to enjoy a slimming, tasty and filling way of eating without having to think about counting the calories.

Counting the cost

It's a common conception that the cost of healthy eating is prohibitively expensive. It need not be. While some food retailers do charge a premium for 'healthier' items, such as wholemeal bread, not all do. And there is no need to make use of modified food products such as low-calorie, slimmers TV dinners or calorie-counted ready meals and recipe dishes. Seasonal vegetables and fruit, oily fish, bread, pasta, potatoes, rice and dried pulses are some of the cheapest (and most filling) foods available, and they make up the bulk of your new way of eating. Plenty of store cupboard staples such as canned tomatoes and even beans are relatively cheap and make the basis of tasty dishes.

In cases of difficulty ...

If you want to change and try hard, but do not make any progress, then maybe you need some professional support. Consider asking your GP for a referral to a counsellor or a dietitian. If you find that you are depressed and therefore unable to motivate yourself to make the changes you would like, ask your GP to refer you to a psychologist. If money difficulties are preventing your progress, approach your local social services department.

Winning Through Summary

Strategies for coping with changing your diet:
- Do it with a friend or the family.
- Think positively of all the good foods you can eat.
- Find a reason for really wanting to do it.
- Talk to someone when the going gets tough.
- Recognise danger times and places.
- Be assertive – explain clearly and calmly what you want to eat or drink.

Glossary

ANTIOXIDANT Substance that delays or prevents oxidation. Oxidation makes butter go rancid and metal go rusty. In foods, oxidisation produces damaging free radicals (see below) as a by-product of normal cell life (ie respiration, or the burning of oxygen). So called oxidative stress can initiate heart disease (see cholesterol) and cancer.

ANTIOXIDANT NUTRIENTS Nutrients with antioxidant powers include vitamins C, E and beta carotene, probably other carotenoids (see below), and minerals such as zinc, selenium, copper and manganese. There are others and probably some yet to be discovered.

CAROTENOIDS Pigments ranging in colour from red through orange to yellow that are found in plant foods, insects, birds and other plant-eating animals, including humans. There are more than 650 carotenoids. Beta carotene is the most widely available. In the body it can be turned into vitamin A, and it is also an active antioxidant (see above), helping to prevent heart disease and cancer.

CHOLESTEROL A fat-like substance that is made in the body, and contained in animal foods. One of the main causes of heart disease is high levels of blood cholesterol. Eating too much saturated fat can raise blood cholesterol levels. The 'good' type of cholesterol, HDL (high density lipoprotein), carries excess cholesterol to the liver for removal from the body. The 'bad' type, LDL (low-density lipoprotein), deposits oxidised cholesterol on artery walls. Without sufficient antioxidants in the diet to prevent oxidation, this is more likely to happen. Cholesterol deposits make artery walls narrower, increasing the risk of heart disease.

DRV (ALSO LRNI/EAR/RNI) Dietary Reference Values: British government standards for how much of each vitamin and mineral it is thought we need. There are several categories:

EAR (Estimated Average Requirement) Because we are all different, standards have been set for average needs, recognising that some people need more and some less.

RNI (Reference Nutrient Intake) The amount that is enough for virtually everyone, including those with high requirements. The RNI is thought to be higher than most people need, so anyone eating that much of a nutrient is unlikely to be deficient.

LRNI (Lower Reference Nutrient Intake) The amount needed by those for with low needs. If people habitually eat less than the LRNI they will be deficient.

Safe Intake The government's expert panel, which set the DRVs, felt there was not enough information to estimate EARs, RNIs or LRNIs for some substances. They therefore set a 'safe intake' which is judged to be about right for most people's needs, but not so large as to cause undesirable effects.

Fats

MONOUNSATURATED Found mainly in olive oil, groundnut and rapeseed oils, avocados, most nuts and some spreads. Monounstaurated fats may have similar beneficial effects to polyunsaturates (see below). They do not raise blood cholesterol levels. (See Cholesterol.)

POLYUNSATURATED Found in vegetable oils, such as sunflower, soya and corn oil, and in oily fish. Eating sufficient polyunsaturates helps reduce blood cholesterol levels. Polyunsaturates also contain essential fatty acids which the body cannot make, but which are needed for good health.

SATURATED The type of fats found mainly in animal foods such as meat and dairy produce. Other sources are 'hydrogenated vegetable fats and oils' found mainly in hard and some soft margarines and cooking fats. Eating too much saturated fat raises blood cholesterol levels and increases the risk of heart disease.

FREE RADICAL Highly reactive molecule made inside the body and encountered from outside pollutants. Free-radical molecules are one electron short (electrons are usually paired), so they grab an electron from another molecule, disturbing the chemical balance by making another electron a single unit, thus setting up a chain reaction. Free radicals are produced constantly in the body as part of normal functions. They need to be dealt with immediately by antioxidants because they can damage DNA.

MINERAL Inorganic substance needed for normal function of the body (eg calcium). Trace elements are minerals required in minute amounts (eg zinc).

VITAMINS Organic substances needed in small amounts for growth and in normal daily chemistry of the body. It is essential to eat vitamins in food because (with the exception of vitamin D made by the action of sunlight on the skin and vitamin B12 made in the gut from micro-organisms) the body cannot make vitamins.

References

The National Food Guide, Health Education Authority in partnership with the Department of Health and the Ministry of Agriculture, Fisheries and Food, July 1994.

Weaning and The Weaning Diet, COMA (Committee on Medical Aspects of Food Policy) report, HMSO, October 1994.

Nutritional Aspects of Cardiovascular Disease, COMA (Committee on Medical Aspects of Food Policy) report, HMSO, November 1994.

Index